WELCOME TO WYNOTT

RETHINKING THE WAY WE'VE ALWAYS DONE THINGS
RAY HARRIS
with Lily Coyle

WELCOME TO WYNOTT © copyright 2012 by Ray Harris and Lily Coyle.
All rights reserved. No part of this book may be reproduced in any form whatsoever,
by photography or xerography or by any other means, by broadcast or transmission,
by translation into any kind of language, nor by recording electronically or otherwise,
without permission in writing from the author, except by a reviewer, who may quote
brief passages in critical articles or reviews.

Cover Illustration: Kevin Cannon
Book Design and Typesetting: James Monroe Design, LLC.

ISBN 13: 978-1-59298-494-7

Library of Congress Catalog Number: 2012907796

Printed in the United States of America

First Printing: 2012
Second Printing: 2012

16 15 14 13 12   6 5 4 3 2

Beaver's Pond Press, Inc.
7108 Ohms Lane
Edina, MN 55439-2129
(952) 829-8818

BeaversPondPress.com
To order, visit BeaversPondBooks.com
or call (800) 901-3480. Reseller discounts available.

WelcomeToWynott.com

I dedicate this book to my parents:

To my father, Leo, for passing to me his vision and commitment to the community;

To my mother, Eleanor, for instilling in me her creative mind and the courage to follow my dreams and make them a reality.

Contents

Preface vii
Wynott? 1

1: *Where We Are Now 3*
2: *How We Got Here. 22*
3: *Who's in Charge 40*
4: *Who Does the Work 56*
5: *How We Pay for Stuff 61*
6: *How We Get Around 71*
7: *Where We Live 100*
8: *What We Learn 126*
9: *What We Buy 154*
10: *When Does It Get Better? 164*

Acknowledgements 181
About Lily Coyle & Kevin Cannon . . 182

PREFACE

> "Some men see things as they are and ask why.
> I dream of things that never were and ask,
> why not."
>
> ROBERT KENNEDY

That's been the modus operandi for my entire career. In 1950, at the dawn of the baby boom, I came out of Stanford with an industrial psychology degree. I then spent a hitch as an army officer, teaching recruits hand-to-hand combat. My first civilian position was as foreman at a toilet seat factory. These combined experiences inspired me to strike out on my own, sink or swim. For the next fifty-plus years I served as my own boss—and my own employee—making up my job description as I went. It worked out pretty well.

Unfettered by any corporate rules or customs, I've been free to take risks and face challenges, sometimes to succeed, and occasionally to meet failure head-on. I fancy myself a problem-solver, always wondering why we act and live as we do, and what best practices elsewhere might improve our ability to afford and enjoy a better quality of living. Every project I've completed started out as a "why not?"

Why not transform a neglected block into a hip urban retail center? Why not build some tony town homes in the scariest part of the city and bring up the value of the whole neighborhood? Why not open a new middle school that gets kids excited about learning? Why not serve the elderly with a campus designed specifically for their needs? Why not turn an overlooked scrap of land into a downtown dog park? All of these "why nots" came to fruition. And there were "why nots" that never made it off the ground. But each one was an invaluable education unto itself.

A long-standing student of how and where we live, I've spent my career searching for more efficient, cost-effective, and sensible ways to work, to play, to learn, and to survive in our American milieu. I've come away with the firm belief that acknowledgement and management of change significantly improves every aspect of our lives.

When you spend eighty or more years on this planet, you learn a thing or two. Again and again, project after project, I've had to break down irrational fears and push through resistance to change. I've had

PREFACE

to overcome complacency, doubt, and every kind of obstacle you can imagine. I've learned a lot about the urban community specifically and the human condition in general. I've learned enough that I could write a book about it!

Hey . . . why not?

WYNOTT?

In our country, we hear a lot of "Why?"

"Why does it have to be this way?" "Why can't someone come up with something better?" "Why do we keep running into the same problems?"

It is our right and privilege as citizens to grumble and complain about why things are the way things are. But at some point, we need to stop saying "Why?" and start saying "Why not?"

This is that point.

Things *can* be different, things *can* get better, and this book is here to show how it can be done. Borrowing from the U.S. Marines, it's time to adapt, overcome, and improvise. Few of us choose change, but none of us can escape it. Think about what we could do if we were open to change, and had the capacity to prepare for and even to shape it!

Within these pages are some specific instructions for improving our way of life. But more important than any one detail is the all-encompassing idea that this is a book about change. Specifically, this is a book that questions why we show futile resistance to unavoidable change. In particular, we take a look at how our built environment and our way of life have changed and will continue to change.

This book is a study of the savvy management of inevitable change, as applied to the new American urban community.

This new community is called "Wynott."

1

Where We Are Now

WHY DO WE ALLOW CHANGE TO MANAGE US?

Change is the only thing we can rely on. From the microscopic level to the macrocosmic level, everything that we know and experience is in a constant state of flux. Our earth is ever in motion, revolving at a rate of nine hundred miles per hour. By the time you reach the end of this sentence, our planet has traveled another twenty miles in its yearly orbit around the sun. And while our outer world hurtles through an endlessly expanding universe, our inner world is also in motion. Our bodies are in a perpetual state of decay and renewal as our cells die and regenerate themselves. Roughly every seven years we replace most of the cells in our bodies.

The world spins. Time marches on. We grow and we age, and we have no control over any of this, no say in the matter. Which may be why we tend to cling so closely to the matters we feel we *can* control.

If you've ever watched a baby turn into a toddler, you've had the chance to witness the discovery of the ego. It often happens in the high chair. Mom and Dad marvel at how cooperative their wonderful baby is—THIS baby isn't fussy; this baby is curious and eager for new experiences. THIS baby will happily try any fruit or vegetable . . . until one day, Baby learns a new word. Baby learns to say "no." The very same baby, the one who will pick any dirty thing up off the floor and put it into his mouth, will suddenly clam up and refuse to try a lovely new piece of fresh fruit when offered by Mommy.

And it doesn't get much better for us humans from that point onward. The moment we learn "no," we apply the word early and often and we resist as much as possible. We don't care if it's good for us or not. When change is presented to us, we tend to stonewall, no matter the potential outcome. We are naturally distrustful of new ideas. Our natural first reaction is to resist change. Think about the popular strategy of reverse psychology—you can more easily sway someone toward your line of thinking if you can trick them into believing that they are actually refusing to do what you want them to do. We cling like crazy to our present situation, even if it's making us miserable.

The irony is, we resist change because it gives us the illusion of control. But we could experience the *reality* of control by embracing and initiating change instead of simply resisting it.

AN OFFER THEY CAN'T REFUSE

There are some people who do seek change, voluntarily. And most people will be motivated to change if you make them "an offer they can't refuse." That means one of two radical motivators, in gangster speak:

1. Pay them off—lure them in with a big profit-making opportunity.

2. Lean on them—make things so unbearable that they're forced to change.

WELCOME TO WYNOTT

When we human beings are made an offer we "can't refuse," it can lead us to change *what* we are, by evolution; *where* we live, by migration; or *how* we function, by innovation.

When are things so unbearable that we're forced to change? Evolution gives us a clue. Most of our physical features developed as ways for our species to survive in this environment. The ones who failed to adapt have been left behind as artifacts on the path from *Ardipithicus ramidus* to *Homo sapiens*. Adaptation is our greatest survival strategy.

Migration is another. There is no more profound change, within our control, than to leave behind the familiar and strike out to a foreign land, with no guarantee of survival, success, or return.

In the United States, we know that the Native Americans were already here when Westerners arrived and that slaves were brought in by force. Most of the rest of the people who founded our early nation had nothing to live for in their homelands; things were so dire there due to famine, crowding, or persecution that they left everything they knew behind for a harrowing journey to an unknown land, where they fought like hell just to survive. Those who didn't come because of fear came because of opportunity. Land was given away to people willing to cultivate it. For the average immigrant to America in the 1800s, it was the chance of a lifetime.

WHERE WE ARE NOW

For immigrants from the beginning of our nation until the present day, it is the same story. They come because it's unbearable in their homeland, or else because there's opportunity here that they can't find anywhere else.

Innovation is another impetus to change. When someone comes up with something new, be it fire, the wheel, the printing press, the atom bomb, or the personal computer, it forces a watershed transformation in the way we live. Innovation is not just things, of course. It's also ideas, like systems and organizations—religions, for instance. Whatever your age, countless innovations have come to prominence in your own lifetime, transforming the way you live, and you seldom think twice about them. Cable television, Velcro, cell phones, personal computers, the Internet, hand sanitizer, high-fructose corn syrup, Facebook, ibuprofen, debit cards, and juice boxes were all unheard of forty years ago, and today they permeate our lives. There's no way to guarantee what the next big thing will be or how it will transform humankind, but we *can* guarantee that something new will always come along. And like adaptations and migrations, an innovation typically succeeds because it creates an opportunity or solves a problem.

A key component to innovation, migration, and even adaptation is leadership. Some bold soul always has to show the others how much better it can be and rally followers to do the same. One fish had to crawl out of the water first and adapt to land to show it could be done. One courageous explorer had to travel into the wilderness or over the seas, migrate away from the familiar into the unknown, and lead others onward. And any innovation will founder and fizzle in its early stages if it doesn't have a champion convincing others to try it—a leader starting a movement. Somebody has to move that invention out of the garage, demonstrate it, explain it, manufacture it, and then market it. What innovations have been lost throughout history because of a lack of leadership? How many people have come up with great new ideas, but have not had the courage or the charisma to get them out to the world?

Adaptation, migration, and innovation lead to the exciting stuff: the stuff that history is made of, the times when things get better. But we don't have to wait for things to become unbearable or for some once-in-a-lifetime opportunity in order to make things better. All we really need are some talented leaders to show us the way. We just need to find them.

Lots of people have ideas. And you don't have to go far to find people who have a lot to say about how much better it could be. Go to any college campus. Any rock concert. Ask anyone from roughly age fifteen to twenty-five. They'll tell you how bad things are and how much better they can be. They'll tell you to question authority and fight the power. They've got some strong ideas and a ton of energy.

This energy is powerful and exciting, but the problem is, the young people shouting for change are mostly the ones in the worst position to make it. They're on the lowest rungs of their career ladders. They often don't own property. They have little influence, little authority, and not much holding them down—no house payments, no kids, no real careers yet to speak of. The main thing young people have is passion.

It would be great if we could all hang onto that passion as we advance through life, gaining power at work, building influence and authority. However, as soon as we've got a little something to hang onto, a little something to watch over, our tendency is to conform to society's expectations. In other words, exactly when we reach the point where we have the power and the clout to really change things, we lose interest in causing change. Why is this?

Certainly, once we get a piece of the pie, we want to protect it. But it's more than that. By the time we reach that stage of life we've endured a lot of disheartening rejection. We've beaten our heads against quite a few walls, and didn't like it. From our earliest years, peer pressure forces us either to conform or to hide our true selves, lest we face consequences. We learn this fact at school, at church, in our neighborhoods, at work, in the military, or in any group we find ourselves inhabiting.

We're told by everyone—our parents, our teachers, our bosses, our leaders—to toe the line. At some point it sinks in. We obey. And so we become subservient.

We are subservient all up and down the chain of command. We learn subservience as the way to survive the machinations of any institution, and our lives are structured by one institution after another. Whether we are the lowest-ranking member or the highest, we are beholden to some interest other than our own.

Risk-aversion exists at the highest levels. Take a look at the leaders of our corporations. Some CEOs become too fearful of losing a bonus to make bold decisions and exhibit true leadership. A true leader has to make difficult and unpopular decisions that may cause short-term pain in order to bring long-term gain, but the short term is all that seems to matter in these times. If the quarterly earnings aren't going up, up, up, that CEO could be out on his duff, because he is beholden to the shareholders. Most shareholders are only focused on the bottom line—if the bottom line isn't in top shape, they'll just ditch their shares and find a better

WHERE WE ARE NOW

investment. This puts those with the weakest loyalty to an organization in charge of steering the ship, and from the top to the bottom, very few people want to rock the boat. Visionary plans and daring ideas are watered down in committee. Organizations grow too big to be nimble or to stay relevant.

In politics it is the same. A candidate must make so many compromises just to get elected and stay elected that it is impossible to achieve any real goals. He or she is too terrified to make unpopular decisions—and should be. Every breath is monitored by opinion polls. The polls run their lives.

And polls run our personal lives. Everything we want to do seems to require approval from somebody else. We lose our appetite for risk and adventure, because when we fight authority, authority always wins. We get tired of questioning, resisting. There are so many rules to keep track of, so many ways to fail, so many pitfalls that we just duck and cover as best we can.

There's an old trick that farmers use to tame a bull. When the bull is still a tiny calf, the farmer will pick it up and carry it around as often as possible until it grows too big. It's not long before the bull is mighty enough to trample the farmer, but in the bull's mind, that farmer still has the power to pick him up and carry him around. That makes the farmer the boss. We do the same thing to ourselves. We still fear the authority of our younger days, even after we surpass that authority. By the time we reach the height of our powers, we've allowed ourselves to be tamed.

And whether we once raged against the machine or marched to the beat of a different drum, or just dreamed of being something other than what we are now, we've let it go. It's too much work to keep up that level of resistance. Who has the time and the energy? We are complacent, because it's just plain easier. We get in a rut and stay in a rut, and we call it comfort. The hell we know is better than the hell we don't know. Why rock the boat? Things could be worse. It's so much easier to just wind down and settle into complacent inertia.

> **We get in a rut and stay in a rut, and we call it comfort.**

So we give up on changing, on trying to make a difference. We actually spend more time and effort resisting change than we do trying to direct it. And most of us simply ignore it. *Que será, será.* Let the others make the plans. What's the point? Nothing *really* changes anyway.

By doing nothing at all, by approaching life with a laissez-faire philosophy, we're not preventing change. We're simply allowing it to happen willy-nilly.

Because everything DOES change. Everything.

Think about that.

Things are gonna keep changing, so we may as well acknowledge it and have a say. Whether we're younger and filled with passion, older and filled with experience, or somewhere in between, we've got far more power than we realize. So . . .

WYNOTT MANAGE CHANGE?

When you expect things to change, it's not so hard to figure out what you really want and to work to make that happen. Imagine you live in a place where change is a normal part of life, and it is planned for as surely as the sun and the rain and the wind and the snow. For the sake of our story, we're going to call this new neighborhood "Wynott."

WHY WYNOTT?

Because it works. It satisfies. It's the most logical and fulfilling arrangement for a human community.

Prove it? Okay.

How about this: People who've lived on a college campus usually remember that time as being incredibly rich and satisfying—possibly the highlight of their lives—even though they may have been dateless, broke, and sleep-deprived. What's so great about that time of life? (Besides being independent for probably the first time ever, not to mention at the peak of one's physical perfection?)

What's great is being surrounded by peers, especially a diverse group of peers involved in endlessly different associations, teams, clubs, organizations, and groups. What's great is learning and thinking about the

future and being exposed to a constant stream of new information, ideas, and possibilities. What's great is being able to walk or bike to nearly everything—classes, meals, bookstores, the clinic, the chapel, the gym, and various hangouts. What's great is running into pals, or making new pals, anywhere on campus. What's great is signing up for work-study opportunities that make it possible to put sweat equity toward the cost of living. What's great is the enduring bonds and friendships formed while navigating the close quarters of a dorm room or other shared housing.

Those bonds and friendships mean that those who grasp organic chem or Beowulf are often willing to tutor those who don't. Those who have cars on campus are often willing to give lifts to those who don't. Those who have TVs and game consoles are often willing to open up their rooms to those who don't. Those who

WHERE WE ARE NOW

have family nearby are often willing to play host and tour guide to those who don't.

Many of these patterns are also found on military bases, aboard ships, or in any place that brings a diverse group of people together to build community while using resources as efficiently and conveniently as possible.

These patterns are what make Wynott a satisfying place to live, at any age:

- Constant learning, new ideas, and possibilities

- The sense of a wide-open future

- A community filled with familiar faces, as well as a diversity of interests, goals, and abilities

- Everything handy, within walking or biking distance

- Alternative ways to defray the cost of living by way of sweat equity

- An efficient density of housing that saves money, fosters neighborliness, and builds trust

- The voluntary sharing of resources, transportation, goods, knowledge, connections, and other intangible valuables

Wynott is a lot like that rich and satisfying campus experience, but without the final exams.

WHERE IS WYNOTT?

Well, where do you live? Wynott might be an inner-city neighborhood, an aging suburb, or a small town. It might be defined as a high-school district or a municipality. Wynott might be an area defined by physical boundaries, such as a river on one side, a highway on the other.

It's entirely possible to paint a thick purple borderline around Wynott to indicate that things are just a little bit different on the inside. Possible. But not a requirement.

Wynott is small enough for you to run into folks you know, yet big enough to be its own entity with a healthy mix of shops and businesses. Wynott is home to a variety of people of different ages, household types, and socioeconomic standing. Some of these people are students, some are retirees. Some are in the trades, some are professionals, some are artists, some are self-employed, and some are homemakers. Each Wynott has its own flavor. Maybe it's a company town or a tourist town. Maybe there's a high concentration of seniors or of one particular ethnic group. While there isn't conformity, there is camaraderie.

WHO LIVES IN WYNOTT?

Whatever the makeup, in Wynott there are three kinds of people: those who lead, those who follow, and those who get out of the way. Any person in Wynott might fill any of those roles at any given time—sometimes following, sometimes leading—but everyone in Wynott understands that without talented, trusted leadership there's no adaptation, migration, or innovation. Leadership is a difficult, uphill climb—both ways. And when someone is called to lead in Wynott (as many are) they can count on support. This refers to leaders, not dictators. Real leaders take the needs of others and the good of the community into account, accept input, consider all factors, and act in the best interests of the group. Wynott cultivates and supports this kind of leadership. While healthy debate is always encouraged, in Wynott it's *not* okay to stonewall and naysay just for the sake of stonewalling and naysaying.

Wynott is simply a place where people have agreed to try something different, and enough people have committed to make it work. But you could live in Wynott and not play the game. Participation is not mandatory. You could live in the next district over and still be great friends with Wynott, because it's not a competition. It's just a fresh perspective. It's the idea that citizens can work together to guide change instead of getting left in the dust when the inevitable changes run them over.

Yeah, but—

Yeah, but we can't change the laws and we don't have enough money and we're never gonna get everyone to agree to go along with this—we can't even agree on where to put the lawn chairs for the block party!

Don't worry about that. It's easier than you'd think.

WHAT IS WYNOTT?

Wynott is the voluntary and democratic act of working with what we've got to improve our quality of life in measurable ways.

See? Told you it was easy. Consider these guiding principles:

1. **Wynott works with what's possible within the existing system.** Don't worry, for now, about trying to change the laws of your community, your state, or your nation. There's not much

WHERE WE ARE NOW

need for new legislation, although legislation may eventually and spontaneously be inspired by Wynott. The first deal is that we do the best we can to work with what we've got. Bloom where we're planted. Start making lemonade out of lemons. It *is* possible to have a different lifestyle, and a different perspective, without making huge changes in the law.

2. Wynott doesn't need special funding. We may not control the financial decisions made at state and federal levels, but we can be savvier with the money that we are entitled to use. Wynott says, "Give us what we're entitled to, no more, no less, and let us handle it." Wynott simply does a better job with the funding that's already designated to run the community by taking the same budget and looking at it differently. Starting as a revenue-neutral project, Wynott sets a plan in motion to create efficiencies that will save money over the long run. Squeezing everything we can out of the assets we've already got will both eliminate waste and curb unnecessary new spending. It's important to consider the lifecycle costs of any venture, not just the outlay costs. Some quality-of-life issues do require additional expenditures or larger up-front expenditures, and that option is always on the table. Changes take time, like any tree, to reach fruition. Wynott is not about instant gratification, quarterly reports, and short-term results. Wynott looks farther ahead than the next election. Wynott requires vision—vision that will pay off, and cost less, over time.

3. **Wynott isn't Left or Right.** It's everywhere. It can work for conservatives and liberals, urbanites and suburbanites, the affluent and the underfunded. Basically, it covers any group of people that might be into food and shelter. There's no dictator, and it's not autocratic. The governance of Wynott must be practical and possible while maintaining the power of democracy.

4. **Wynott isn't telling anybody what to do.** That includes residents of Wynott as well as neighboring communities. The Wynott environment is not competitive, but rather supportive of and cooperative with adjacent communities. As they succeed, so succeeds Wynott.

5. **Wynott produces measurable results.** "Maybe not today, and maybe not tomorrow, but soon, and for the rest of your life." Intellectually

and intuitively, we know we can do better. There are subjective goals and quality-of-life issues, which can't really be measured. Expect to notice a lot of that happening in Wynott. But don't think it's all just feel-good Happy-O-Meter stuff. We are implementing changes that are subject to real analysis and accountability to demonstrate that we're doing a better job. As the efficiencies and improvements are integrated, our value goes up. Expect to see a measureable increase in the value of our time, the value of our spending dollars, and the value of our properties.

With these five sensible guidelines in our hip pocket, there's only one thing left to learn:

HOW DOES WYNOTT WORK?

Wynott works by applying fresh thinking to all existing systems and structures.

Now don't let the all-encompassing totality of that concept frighten you. The first step is a doozy, but once we get going, it soon becomes a way of life. It's just a simple matter of systematically changing the "Why?" to "Wynott!"

2

How We Got Here

WHY ARE THINGS THE WAY THEY ARE NOW?

From the very beginning, human beings have been social creatures. Even the Bible says, "It is not good that man should be alone." The first social system we built was tribalism, and it has had a very adaptive effect on human evolution. Tribalism, for better or worse, is still in existence, in various forms, making it the longest-lasting societal structure to date. When individuals do leave their "tribe," it's usually to find or to build a new one.

HOW WE GOT HERE

Consider the American pioneers. They entered the wilderness seeking freedom, land ownership, and adventure. Isolated from society, they had to build their own homes, make their own clothes, and hunt and grow their own food. They also had to serve as their own doctors, dentists, teachers, and police officers. It was a grueling life of hardship, and we proudly think of the founders of our land as rugged individuals who knew how to pull themselves up by their bootstraps.

Which they did. And as soon as they got those boots pulled up, they quickly did what human beings have always done to survive—they banded together. The pioneers went from being isolated individuals to living in small settlements to forming small communities. They watched each other's backs, built each other's barns, delivered each other's babies. They traded goods, food, and services. The foundation of our nation may be the Declaration of Independence, but our success is due to cooperation, communication, trade, and *inter*dependence. As people worked together in our nation's early years, communities prospered and grew into small towns, and then larger towns, and then cities.

Cities boomed and flourished—or sometimes went bust—across the United States. Surrounding each city was the country. Urban or rural, those were the choices. If you rode a train from coast to coast, the demarcation was clearly seen through your window. There were no suburbs. Unless it was wilderness, land

was for farming. If you weren't growing crops and feeding others, you didn't have need for much land. And you had no concept of *lawn*. Grass belonged in prairies and pastures. A yard was used to grow edible and medicinal plants or to keep a few animals. The rest of it was usually hard-packed dirt, which was swept clean daily.

But sweeping dirt can get kind of old. By the mid-1800s, the wealthiest Americans began to emulate the European gentry, whose sparkling green lawns were one of the earliest forms of conspicuous consumption. To further differentiate themselves from the peasantry, wealthy European estate owners turned their land into grass, meant only for leisure—no grazing allowed. Acres and acres of manicured lawn, a high-maintenance crop that served no purpose and fed no one, was the ultimate status symbol and the highest form of luxury.

A European-style lawn wasn't possible for most Americans, until the push mower was invented in 1870, and until the garden hose and running water became widely available. Even then, it wasn't until the 1930s that a suitable mix of lawn grass was developed to grow in our climate. The moment it did, the Garden Club of America (GCA) took over. According to Virginia Scott Jenkins in *The Lawn: A History of an American Obsession*, the GCA launched a beautification campaign to convince homeowners that it was their civic duty to maintain a beautiful lawn, which was described in pamphlets as "a single type of grass with no intruding weeds, kept mown at a height of an inch and a half, uniformly green, and neatly edged." Americans fell in line, and fell in love—with their lawns. To own a home with a patch of green grass was to truly own an estate.

Lost on the average homeowner was the fact that a genuine estate could, and did, employ teams of laborers to maintain its lawns. For the gentry, a lawn is a carefree place to spend leisure time. For everybody else, leisure time is spent caring for lawns. To this day, average American homeowners proudly discharge their own lawn duties and spend their precious little free time seeding, feeding, weeding, watering, and mowing a small green acreage. The sparkling green lawn is still the most enduring symbol of the American dream.

The GCA had only just cinched its victory over American yards when World War II came to a close. The GIs returned from war with VA loans to buy houses, and everyone wanted an estate of their own, with a green lawn to mow. Oh, and a big garage for the family car. For now we had a lot of cars. We had factories freed up from war work to put them together. We had access to raw materials from which to build them, and we had cheap gasoline with which to run them. We also had pent-up purchasing demand with which

HOW WE GOT HERE

to buy them, after years of depression and war, and we had the Federal-Aid Highway Act.

Also known as the National Interstate and Defense Act, it was signed into law by President Dwight Eisenhower in 1956 and launched the largest public works project to date in American history. At a cost of $25 billion, 41,000 miles of interstate highways were constructed over twenty years. Eisenhower supported this act because of his own military experience and his conviction that good highways are essential to national defense—that is, to transport troops and goods across the country in the event of an invasion. But instead of preventing an invasion, the new highways fueled an explosion—the explosion of suburban America.

This subsidization of suburban road infrastructure suddenly made commutes between urban centers much faster, enabling the growth of suburbs in rings around the city. As service sector jobs began replacing industrial jobs, many factories were shuttered, leaving large gaps downtown. At the same time, skyscrapers rose downtown, and real estate prices inflated, pushing residents out and bringing commercial tenants in. The city center became a clearly defined and clearly zoned business center, its former residents left looking for somewhere to live.

GIs who came home to isolated farms or crowded urban environments were drawn to the suburbs for many reasons. With VA loans at an unheard of 3 percent interest, they'd have been fools not to buy, and it made no sense to resist the incentives to fill the suburbs, the most logical and attractive location for growing families.

The need for housing was real. Very little had been built during the Great Depression. During World War II, even fewer homes had been built, due to a scarcity of raw materials as well as laborers. Everything and everyone had been needed for the war effort.

During the war, one innovative Navy SeaBee named William Levitt paid close attention to the mass-production techniques used to build military housing. When he returned home again to work with his father and brothers' custom home-building firm, he preached the gospel of uniform and interchangeable parts and quickly converted his entire family. Levitt & Sons

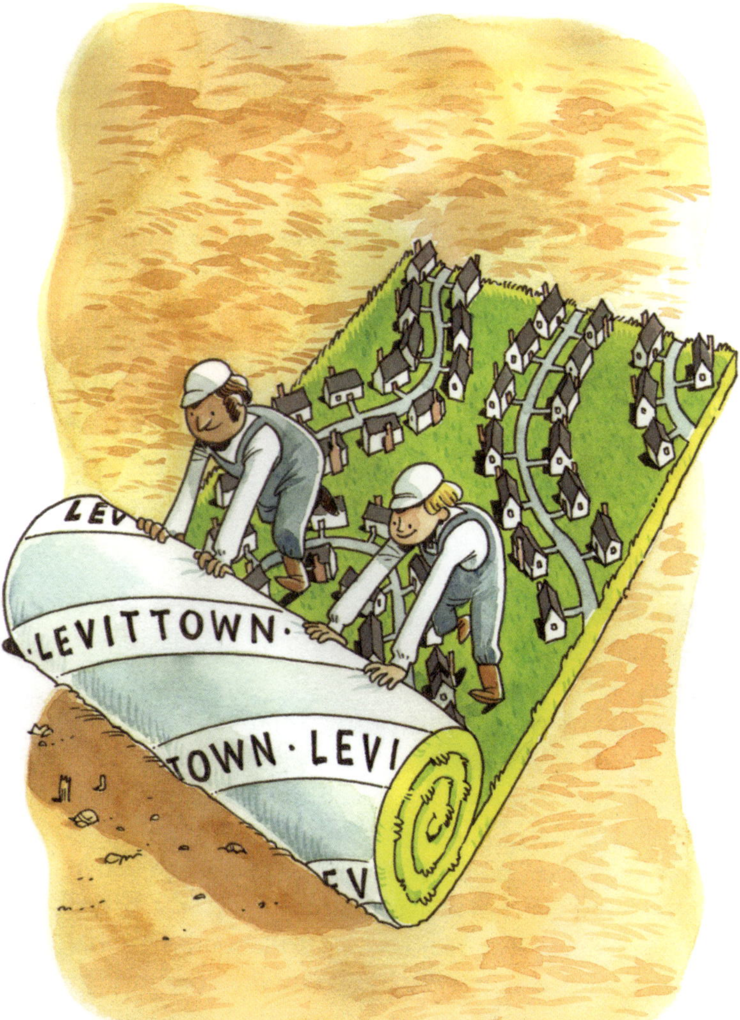
LEV
·LEVITTOWN·
TOWN · LEVI
EV

designed efficient blueprints and perfected cost-effective construction techniques, anticipating the postwar boom. They were able to increase speed and cut costs by leaving unfinished "expansion attics" for the owners to complete. They used precut lumber, and negotiated a change in the building code to allow building on concrete slabs. They hired nonunion contractors.

In 1948 they boasted a production rate of thirty houses per day. With surging demand, and with the Federal Housing Agency's support, the Levitt firm began offering thirty-year mortgages with no money down and monthly house payments that rivaled renting. And as fast as they were building homes, it just wasn't fast enough.

Their Levittown developments in New York, Pennsylvania, New Jersey, and Puerto Rico started a rage and set the standard for postwar planned communities. Heavy advertising pushed the American Dream, emphasizing the good life in the suburbs. The homeowners who rushed to live in Levittown and other developments focused on the positive aspects of their new homes: large lots, large yards, houses pulled back from the streets, and winding roads that meandered in soft curves, which made it harder to notice the lack of sidewalks. The average house was 1,100 square feet and had a detached garage, no basement, no air conditioning, and one bathroom. Families with three kids, five kids, and more filled up these ranch homes, mowed the lawns, and washed their cars in the driveways.

The Levittown model wasn't the only model. Tonier suburbs with wider lots, more generous square footage, and more elaborate models to choose from lured those who weren't reliant on a VA loan or no money down. They simply offered an escape from the close confines of the noisy, dirty city. They also offered every possible modern amenity, and so the affluent began packing.

Many of those who could afford to get out of the city took all of their money and left. When the first wave left, the second wave saw the writing on the wall and followed. The bulk of those who remained behind were too poor, too old, too infirm, or too not-white to make it out to the suburbs. For them, suburbanization was a huge step backwards.

Mixed-race cities quickly unmixed, thanks to white flight. Mortgage discrimination and racially restrictive covenants meant that the white areas got whiter, in suburbs that belonged exclusively to them. But anyone of any race who *could* get out of the city, did, taking all of their tax dollars with them.

Some had no choice but to stay, even after their own homes were bulldozed. When neighborhoods had to be leveled for highway construction, the ones that disappeared were poor and minority communities. Homeowners were evicted from previously stable neighborhoods and paid non-negotiable lowball prices in the name of eminent domain. With nowhere to go and little money to get there, many of the people who lived in the interstate's path were boxed up into housing projects.

Houses in no danger of being bulldozed still lost value as they were turned into multiplexes or left vacant. The houses' new residents had fewer resources to care for the properties, and the landlords who bought them up had no incentive to *keep* them up; they made the least investment necessary to stay profitable.

This large-scale decentralization left a small island of skyscrapers in the middle, a big donut of suburbs sprawling out beyond, and miles of depleted neighborhoods in between, hidden behind the tall walls of the interstate that served commuting suburbanites. With the tax-paying earners gone and mostly the needy left behind, the city, drained of vitality, began to buckle under its burden. The worse the city seemed, the worse it became; and the better the suburbs looked in comparison.

There was a tremendous push to build new houses to meet the suburban demand, even as existing housing stock sat unused in city neighborhoods. Increasing population and changing demographics forced expansion, and developers gave the people what they wanted. More or less.

Building firms could have developed land in or near the city, where the sewers and the infrastructure already existed. But raw land, unserved by roads and utilities, was much cheaper farther out. So out they went, snapping up low-priced potato fields. The small farm towns, however, were not prepared to fund the large suburban developments growing within their boundaries. They could not afford to provide infrastructure like sewers and water systems, and services like schools and fire departments. Legal complications arose when some developments sprawled across municipal boundary lines.

Eventually the federal government stepped in. The new highways were already funded, but now grant programs and revolving loan funds were set up to subsidize development away from the cities. Billions of federal dollars were made available for waste-water systems, the majority of it earmarked to build new infrastructure. This gave metropolitan areas incentive to keep building farther and farther out, even as they struggled to fund the maintenance and operation of the infrastructure already in place. It's the same kind of logic in play when your credit card is maxed out, so you apply for a new one.

While the government subsidized suburban infrastructure and highways, the private sector played a part as well. In dense urban areas, it costs much less, per capita, to provide utilities such as phone, gas, electric, water, and waste-water services. A telephone landline, for instance, costs the least to operate in the central business district. It costs twice as much in the rest of the central city and ten times as much in the urban fringe. But average price costing means that everyone pays the same rate, even though the urban fringe is significantly raising the price paid by the rest of the metropolitan area. Average pricing policies were developed to lower the burden on farmers, back when phones were few and far between and the entire nation was more or less divided into purely rural or purely urban areas. But today, average cost pricing is another way that the urban dwellers subsidize the suburbs, making them artificially more affordable.

There's a price to be paid for building and maintaining the suburbs. But it isn't necessarily being paid by those who live there.

There's a price to be paid for building and maintaining the suburbs. But it isn't necessarily being paid by those who live there.

Public transportation is another expense that doesn't accurately reflect the cost of suburban living. A commuter who lives within the city limits might pay the same fare to ride a mile as the suburban commuter pays to ride ten miles. The passenger who uses the least amount of fuel is subsidizing everyone else.

HOW WE GOT HERE

As Americans drove new cars to private estates, investment shifted away from public transportation. Rugged individualists and aspiring gentry simply don't take streetcars. In fact, streetcars move way too slowly and take up way too much room. These incredibly safe, efficient, and egalitarian transportation systems were dismantled to make room for more cars and to allow those cars to travel at higher and higher speeds. Streetcars were replaced by noisy, exhaust-chugging buses. Soon the streets were cleared of pedestrians, bicyclists, and anything other than gas-guzzling automobiles—great big cars, great big buses.

From a passenger perspective, buses were fairly comfortable and easy enough to manage, but in a car society, the bus soon became known as the poor man's ride in most urban areas. If you didn't own a car, there must be something wrong with you. As it became stigmatized, support for public transit dwindled. The commerce it had supported also faded.

The thriving shops and businesses that had once clustered along streetcar lines declined. Many failed. Many more packed up and moved out to the promising new shopping malls in the suburbs. The city held fewer shopping, entertainment, and service options for those who lived there. For those who didn't, there were fewer reasons to be in the city for anything other than work, and if you were there to work, you got in and got out as quickly as possible—back to the suburbs.

Where our lawns were getting greener.

During WWII, we built ten new munitions plants in the middle of the country to produce ammonium nitrate for bombs. When the war ended, we no longer needed the bombs, but the production capacity was in place, so we switched gears—literally—and put the munitions plants to work developing chemical fertilizers. From bombs to lawns. The Department of Agriculture pushed these cheap and readily available fertilizers on farmers as well as homeowners.

Chemical fertilizers made it easier to grow corn and soybeans in a monoculture, meaning farmers could focus on just a few cash crops instead of diversifying. They no longer relied on crop rotation to manage their soil fertility. But the more crops they produced, the less cash those crops were worth. As farming became more automated, farmers became less necessary. Many sold out or were forced out, creating a glut. Acres and acres of devalued farm fields became green-lawned housing developments.

Like some sort of Frankensteinian experiment, the suburbs have sucked all of the best resources away from city and country alike to create a way of life that somehow fails to provide the vitality or the charm of either. While a city, by nature, brings people together, a suburb, by design, pushes them apart. The suburban front yard is meant for show; it has no porch from which to sit and wave to neighbors walking past. And our acres of grass crop feed no one.

> We're just as isolated as the pioneers, but with none of their survival skills.

We have devolved from people who value cooperation, communication, trade, and interdependence to people who sit alone behind privacy fences in climate-controlled houses watching sensationalized news stories that make us terrified of our own neighbors. We're just as isolated as the pioneers, but with none of their survival skills. We do, however, have much, much greener lawns.

WYNOTT MAKE THINGS BETTER?

We've reached a new era. In their 2011 pamphlet titled "The New American Lawn," the Garden Club of America exhorts homeowners to mow less (three inches will do), water less (a dormant brown mid-summer lawn is no big deal), ditch the chemical pesticides and fertilizer (dandelions aren't worth the fuss), and incorporate native plants into the landscape ("Mother Nature abhors a monoculture!"). The uniformly green inch-and-a-half days are over.

Everything is changing, not just the lawn. Everything about our way of life is different. We've got more choices than we've ever had before—if we take the time to see what they are. It's pretty exciting!

In Wynott we don't sit around and bellyache. We get off our duffs and do something. About everything.

We start with good **leadership**. By making it an honor to serve the people of Wynott, we attract the most honorable people into service. There's a tremendous emphasis on **volunteerism**; we depend on it to make Wynott flourish. We generate positive peer pressure to encourage it, but more than that, we find ways to offer volunteers tangible incentives and rewards.

One of these rewards comes in the form of community currency, which is a powerful way to keep our local economy vital.

With honorable leadership, a robust stream of volunteerism, and healthy circulation of community currency, Wynott builds the foundation for improving every other aspect of the community, including transportation, the built environment, education, and many others. Every single system and structure is a candidate for the application of fresh thinking.

And as a community we are connected not just in real space, but also in cyberspace. Using a social network—Facebook or something like it—Wynott is linked together by a forum in which everyone can offer ideas, seek help, or get information. Leaders are tuned in to what people are thinking. People can give feedback instantly. This technology is a cheap and efficient way to keep everyone involved, informed, and connected.

We look at our available resources and see where we can do better. We think ahead and plan ahead, not just for the next quarter, but for the next quarter of a century and beyond. In Wynott we have a vision, and we find the right people to see it through.

3

Who's in Charge

WHY WOULD ANY SANE PERSON WANT THIS JOB?

We think of our elected officials as our leaders—which they are. But the job requirements have changed dramatically from those first laid out by our founding fathers. There was a time when vision, character, and judgment were the essential traits of a successful candidate. In today's twenty-four-hour instant newsfeed, the ideal contender on the campaign trail would be a sociopath, a martyr, or a billionaire.

A sociopath has the narcissism to endure and actually enjoy the unending public scrutiny of candidacy, in which everywhere you go, someone has a cellphone camera ready to catch you with your finger in your nose. Or your kid drinking a beer. Or your spouse having a bad hair day. A sociopath can promise anything to anyone in order to raise the oodles and oodles of money required to mount a campaign. Once that money is there, a sociopath, incapable of empathy, can blithely assassinate opponents in the media. Sociopaths have the grandiose sense of self needed to toot their own horn all day, every day, on a campaign trail that starts about two weeks after the last election and never seems to end. A sociopath has the glibness and superficial charm necessary to spout clever sound bites at will for the short-attention-span electorate. Sociopaths are convincing liars and will say whatever it takes to move themselves forward, making campaign promises and special-interest alliances with ease. Sociopaths have the strong desire for power that will sustain them throughout the grueling election process.

Martyrs will put themselves and their families through that same gauntlet because some voice in their heads tells them that they are on the right path. Martyrs are so strongly called to serve, so solid in their convictions, that they heroically enter the campaign arena and do what must be done to survive the lions. None of them get out unbloodied. They believe in their hearts that they're on the narrow path of the righteous, that they have a higher calling—and sometimes, sometimes, we see it too, and sometimes we even agree with them. But it doesn't mean we call off the lions.

Billionaires simply have the money to drown out the opposition with a bigger, badder shock-and-awe media blitz. And if they don't get the job, that's okay, because they've still got billions of dollars.

Now and then there's a billionaire who also happens to be a sociopath or a martyr, and there's just no stopping that campaign!

Given this field of contenders, we voters have to figure out from the nauseating and incessant coverage which of the candidates are truly willing to serve us, and which are only using us to serve their own desire for power.

> If you're not a sociopath, a martyr, or a billionaire, you gotta wonder why anyone would put themselves through an election.

If you are not a sociopath, a martyr, or a billionaire, you gotta wonder why anyone would put themselves through an election. It's hell on you, hell on your family, and hell on the rest of us who are forced to watch the torturous, demoralizing nonstop coverage. The money doesn't compare to what you could make in the private sector. The job security is lousy. You'll be hated by roughly half of the people you represent. The people who don't hate you and did vote for you

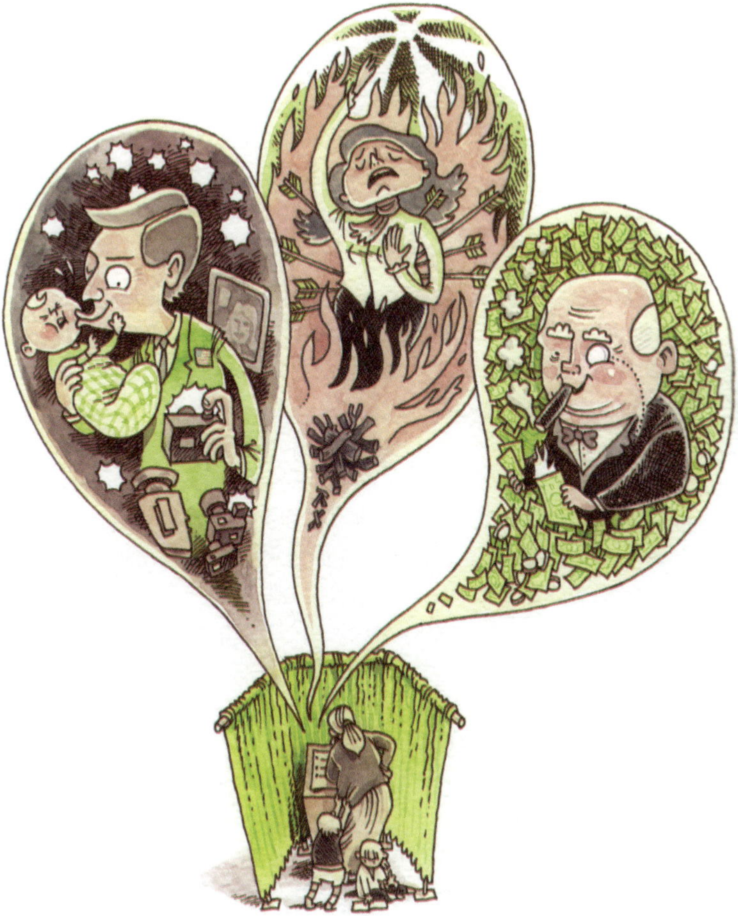

WELCOME TO WYNOTT

will start bellyaching about you before you even attend your first session. You are hamstrung by the demands of fund-raising and by the realities of gridlock, special interests, lobbyists, the media, and ever-increasing air-travel complications.

The typical career path for many of our political leaders (the ones who aren't billionaires) starts with a low-level municipal office, in the trenches. These very important positions are seen as little more than internships on the way to bigger, better things, and the pay and the job descriptions bear that view out. The average council member is a glorified coffee-fetcher, paid peanuts to hear nonstop complaints about garbage pickup, fallen tree branches, stop signs, and potholes. These tedious to-do lists suck up all of their hours, and there is absolutely no time, no support, and no reward for creating and instituting any kind of vision for their city or district. There's no credit given for thinking beyond the boundaries of one's own ward. The job is just not set up to allow real leadership, or true vision, to flourish.

From that entry-level council position all the way up to the president, being an elected official in this country is a hideous, thankless, fruitless, draining job.

Yet we expect people with vision, character, and judgment to pursue it. Here's a little secret—people with vision can see what a bummer it is, people with character don't want to put their family through it, and people with judgment have the sense to find a better job in the private sector. Does that mean that our government is a failure? No.

> "Indeed, it has been said that democracy is the worst form of government except all those other forms that have been tried from time to time."
>
> WINSTON CHURCHILL

Democracy is A-O-K. Nothing wrong with it. What's wrong with democracy in this country is the depth and breadth of the nation it governs and our constant demand for fresh, juicy news content. We've just gotten too darn big and unruly. The bigger a group gets, the broader its mission becomes, and soon the tyranny of the majority waters down the goals of the organization and renders it ineffectual. Leadership becomes nothing more than a glorified game of King of the Hill. Those who manage to fight and claw their way to the top must spend their entire term fending off those who would topple them and take their place. Nothing gets achieved. The only goal is to put someone onto or take someone off of the hill. No real person can lead in these circumstances; every last shred of energy is spent on survival.

And it's not exactly survival of the fittest. When local elections are funded by special interests on the other side of the United States and scrutinized by the national media—when it costs millions of dollars just to get your name on the board—when a candidate must be perpetually "on" and ready with a pithy sound bite—we're no longer looking for normal human beings. We're looking for freaks.

WYNOTT LET LEADERS BE REAL?

In Wynott we like our democracy small. Intimate. Manageable. There can be no King of the Hill, because there is no hill. We keep it sane so that it will attract sane leaders. Most importantly, leadership in Wynott is an honor, and so Wynott is led by honorable people.

Earlier we said that people are guaranteed to change if you make them an offer they can't refuse, which means you either pay them off or you lean on them. Works every time. If you're a gangster.

But if you're not a gangster, you need to be more creative, more inspired—you actually need to lead.

A good leader generates the trust and confidence that cause people to willingly make changes, even if they aren't being paid off or leaned on. A good leader inspires others to contribute and get involved. We might think that these days we suffer a dearth of good leadership, but perhaps we're just not looking in the right places. Maybe it's not the people, but the system.

From every group, someone with the right stuff will emerge. It could be the bold highschooler who first models the new fashion and starts a trend. Or the charismatic neighbor who organizes the block meetings and somehow makes everyone excited about getting together to discuss boulevard maintenance. Or the boss who truly has your back and cares about your life, who mentors you as you tackle things you wouldn't think to tackle on your own. Or even the online discussion-board moderator who keeps the conversation lively and the discourse civil.

Leaders will emerge if the group is appropriately willing to support them. Not blindly follow, but support. A group might even have a variety of leaders, each with different abilities, who step forward in turn as particular situations demand.

Wynott takes inspiration from these spontaneous leaders, the ones who have a calling. While some may have the chops to helm our nation, in most cases they succeed best in smaller settings, where it's still possible to accomodate all of the cogent realities and personalities and needs in play. In smaller settings, it's possible for the group members to know a leader on a personal level, as a peer, as one of their own.

Big goals. But how to implement such a dream in our cynical, post-irony era?

The key is to compile best practices and to refuse to support an inefficient beast. Also, to stay right-sized. Not too small, not too big. If a Wynott community becomes a huge success and grows, it should be split into something like "Wynott East" and "Wynott West," each with separate governance. East and West share as many resources and efficiencies as possible, but it is CRITICAL that they retain separate identities and don't grow beyond their carrying capacities. Carrying capacity, in Wynott, means, "small enough for you to run into folks you know, yet big enough to be its own entity, with a healthy mix of shops and businesses."

It's entirely possible that Wynott can flourish under or alongside the existing leadership of the community. A forward-thinking mayor, an energetic city council, or other duly elected and appointed civic leaders can incorporate the principles of Wynott into their vision plan. If this is not possible, Wynott will have to set up its own governing body. As stated in the Wynott guidelines, this body works under and within all existing laws and structures. But it has the authority to take that which rightfully belongs to the community and make it better.

Here's one template:

A Vision Council of three rotating members is charged with planning and implementing Wynott's future. Their mission is to apply fresh thinking to all existing systems and structures and to work with what they've got in order to improve quality of life in measurable ways. "What they've got" includes getting creative with untapped resources. For example, cultivating public–private collaborations to provide services, in-kind donations, and funding.

A fourth person, equally important, but in a very different role, is tasked with managing the daily details of Wynott. This person, the Manager, handles pothole complaints and speed-bump requests and all of the other ongoing crises that plague residents. Wynott acknowledges that these details must be handled with efficiency and concern, but not at the expense of big-picture thinking.

Those deep thoughts and grand plans are what the future-minded members of the Vision Council get to do. And they do it. The Manager relieves them of the burden of minutiae, and they are unencumbered by the King of the Hill stress of campaigning, because they don't campaign.

All those interested in either Vision or Managing may submit an application listing their qualifications and stating why they wish to hold that position. The field is open to anyone who's lived in Wynott for at least four years and who possesses demonstrable common sense and a work ethic. They must be at least twenty-five years old, the age at which the human brain is believed to have reached maturity. They must be able to pass a background check and prove themselves able and worthy, but that's it. Political experience is not a liability, but these positions are not intended to serve as low-level stepping-stones on the path of the career politician.

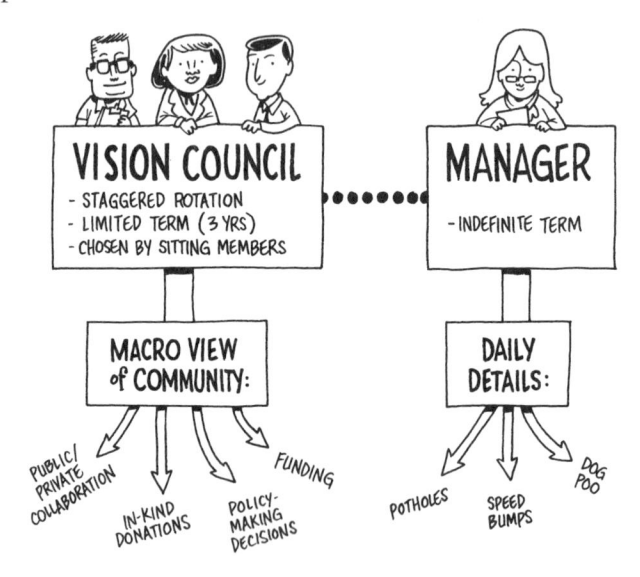

VISION COUNCIL
- STAGGERED ROTATION
- LIMITED TERM (3 YRS)
- CHOSEN BY SITTING MEMBERS

MANAGER
- INDEFINITE TERM

MACRO VIEW of COMMUNITY: PUBLIC/PRIVATE COLLABORATION, IN-KIND DONATIONS, POLICY-MAKING DECISIONS, FUNDING

DAILY DETAILS: POTHOLES, SPEED BUMPS, DOG POO

People with different levels of education and from different walks of life are encouraged to bring their expertise: A stay-at-home mom's credentials are as valid as an attorney's, and an attorney's are as valid as an electrician's. The wider the cross-section of Wynott represented, the better. Diversity of experience and perspective is taken into account as well.

WHO'S IN CHARGE

The Vision Council members serve terms on a staggered rotation. To get this schedule rolling, the inaugural council members, chosen by some outside consultant or committee, will serve terms of two, three, and four years. Subsequent Vision Council members are chosen from the pool of applicants by the sitting members. A new member comes in once a year and an old member goes out. The Manager and the two newest council members choose a replacement for the outgoing council member together.

> People with different levels of education and from different walks of life are encouraged to bring their expertise.

Unless there are no other willing candidates, once a council member has served a term, he or she is ineligible to serve again for at least another five years (ensuring that the sitting group can't keep reelecting themselves). This waiting period also applies to immediate family of outgoing members and those in any other relationship that represents a clear conflict of interest—that is, business partners, employers, roommates, and the like.

The incoming member is announced one month before officially taking the position, and that month is spent shadowing the outgoing member and learning the job. New council members are also enrolled in a training program to learn the realities of governing—how the structure works, the state of the current budget, how everything fits together, what they can and can't do. They get a little tutorial on the difference between exercising vision and picking paint colors. They're brought up to speed on all existing plans and projects. They are not simply given a freshly emptied desk and then left to sink or swim.

During the first ten days of that month, the public has the opportunity to oppose any council member—but there is no vote. There is only a process by which community members may mount a petition making a solid case against the candidate's competence. Should a significant number of Wynott citizens sign to reject the candidate, the member won't be confirmed. Knowing that this can happen, leaders select new council members with care. It is mainly a formality, not unlike the moment in a wedding ceremony when the officiator says, "Speak now or forever hold your peace."

The Manager serves indefinitely, subject to a yearly review by the Vision Council. Whereas rotating the Vision Council members keeps fresh energy and innovative ideas flowing, a talented Manager should be encouraged to keep the job for as long as he or she is motivated to stay, and be rewarded accordingly. Seasoning and experience are important to this position.

The Vision Council and the Manager are assisted by a small staff of local high-school interns who earn credit for providing administrative assistance. The interns may be assigned to do research, update the online community network, make calls, hang signs, take notes, organize meetings and events, do general gopher work, and more. This gives kids an inside look at how their own community is run and involves them directly in meaningful civic affairs. It's also a very efficient use of existing resources.

Unencumbered by the burden of a campaign, and with full awareness of their term limit, the Vision Council is able to make hay during their three years of leadership. They can investigate issues in depth and take time to understand what makes one thing better and something else worse. Without the worries of reelection, they can focus on long-term results and not just immediate return on investment. They can make hard decisions without being punished at the polls.

But that doesn't mean they aren't accountable or have free reign to boondoggle. Wynott leaders are motivated to create a real legacy and to create meaningful change because they live here. Right here. If they get it right, they benefit from the changes they help to enact, along with all of their neighbors. If they screw it up, their neighbors will be giving them grief for the rest of their lives.

People with the vision thing are drawn to lead in Wynott because they actually get to work on the vision thing. And without the obligation of a time-sucking, expensive campaign and all of the false promises it creates, the council isn't thrust into celebrity status. Instead, they get the space to do the job.

Because the pool of leaders comes from within the limited population of Wynott and rotates with regularity, and because anyone who feels called to lead has a reasonable shot, the council members are seen more as peers. This affords them more empathy and cooperation from the public. They are also less vulnerable to the slings and arrows that are regularly hurled at mainstream elected leaders deemed (rightly or wrongly) to be more like celebrities than public servants. A favorite attack-ad accusation of any campaigner is that their opponent is "out of touch" with real people. This just isn't possible in Wynott. We know where you live. We've seen you taking out the trash and walking the dog and picking up the kids from school.

People with the vision thing are drawn to lead in Wynott because they actually get to work on the vision thing.

That's one template. There are other ways to work it. For instance, there could be five members on the Vision Council, if the pool of contenders is deep enough and there's enough passion and interest. The terms could be longer or shorter. Depending on the existing government structure and the needs of Wynott, the Manager may be a part- or full-time paid position. The Vision Council is most likely a part-time position, similar to sitting on a board.

There are also a variety of ways to compensate the Vision Council for their duty. The preferred way, in Wynott, is a graft-proof combination of in-kind benefits and community currency, which will be laid out in coming chapters. Regardless of how leaders are compensated, a key goal of Wynott is to reward people for excellence. However the leadership structure shakes out, as time goes on, more and more former leaders will be part of the community. The wider this pool of alumni gets, the more apparent it becomes that Wynott really is run by the people of Wynott. Pretty soon Wynott will feel a bit like game day in Green Bay, Wisconsin, where everyone walks around full of a shared pride and enthusiasm for the storied NFL team that they, the fans, own. Who knows, maybe the excitement will be so great that Wynott residents will wear something akin to triangular hats of foam-rubber cheese in a show of solidarity. Probably not. But, who knows? Maybe!

4

WHO DOES THE WORK

WHY DO OUR BEST RESOURCES GET PUT OUT TO PASTURE?

Do you have any idea what kind of talent and energy is lying dormant in your community? Take a look, for instance, at senior citizens. Here's a group of people with the longest life expectancy in the history of humankind. They've put about thirty or forty years—that's maybe half of a lifetime—into developing their careers. At the peak of their powers, with a vast accumulation of experience and knowledge, plus access to an extensive network of industry contacts, they're expected to retire, buy an RV, and spend the next twenty years traveling from park to park buying tchotchkes for their grandchildren.

What the hell is that all about?

In every other society, at every other time in history, elders were entrusted to hold the knowledge and the wisdom of the entire community. In America today, they get to hold the shuffleboard paddles. In many cases, not only are they capable and qualified, but their children are grown up and gone, so they have fewer obligations to manage. Many seniors have paid off their houses, and have seen their investments come to fruition. They have the financial wherewithal and the time to work for free, or to work for peanuts. Advances in medicine mean they're healthier and stronger for many years longer than their ancestors. This is a vital, savvy, and energetic group of people who need to be recognized as a resource and called upon to perform.

WYNOTT MAKE THE MOST OF OUR HUMAN RESOURCES?

One of the cornerstones of Wynott USA is more opportunity for community interaction. If you want to retire and play golf every day, that's okay. If you want to crash in front of the TV after work every day, you won't get kicked out. But you will feel like you are missing out. Because in Wynott, people are involved. It's kind of like one of those popular cafes where you bus your own dishes. The food is so good, the crowd is so interesting, and the buzz is so stimulating that you don't mind carrying your dishes to the bus tub and separating out the trash from the glassware. Because you and other customers are willing to do that, the staff can spend more time preparing great food at reasonable prices. And if you just leave your dishes on the table and walk out, someone will handle it. No one is gonna chase you down the street and make you scrape your plate. Odds are, though, that the positive peer pressure will lead most of the patrons to do what's expected and clear their places.

That's how it is in Wynott. You don't have to do your part. But you'll want to, because that's how it works in this community. The structure makes it easy; the peer pressure makes it likely. And incentives, like the chance to earn community currency, make it very attractive. Rewarding people for excellence encourages them to do their best. In Wynott everyone is challenged to find a way to serve where they're willing and able to be at their best. And to move on when it ceases to be motivational.

> You don't have to do your part. But you'll want to, because that's how it works in this community.

The local Wynott grade school, for instance, is run a bit like a co-op. Every parent is expected to sign up for a certain number of volunteer duties that, when spread out over the whole student body, don't mean much more than a few hours per person. Cumulatively, though, they add up to a robust staff of invested families. They can work directly with students, helping in classrooms or lunchrooms or at recess, or they can perform after-hours or weekend tasks, doing maintenance projects, website work, or simple photocopying.

Parents are asked to do this for the benefit of their school and for their own children. For any hours they put in above and beyond the required minimum, they can earn community currency. Anyone else in the community who gives their time to the school will also earn community currency. Retirees are especially welcomed and encouraged to share their knowledge and experience.

And they're not merely welcomed, they are needed. It's happening across the nation. The Baby Boomer generation is hitting retirement age, and the number of children entering school is dropping. Funding is shifting from school budgets to health care. While unemployment numbers are high at the time of this writing, the writing on the wall tells a different story. A giant wave of Americans will soon become senior citizens, and that will transform the unemployment crisis into a labor shortage. It's vital to have efficiencies in place right now to be ready for this shift. That means recruiting and rewarding seniors for volunteering. As the money is pulled out of schools and put into health care, our classrooms can use the help of those seniors who still have so much to offer.

This also means, of course, that as seniors age, more services and volunteers will be needed to help them stay independent. As retirees help the schools, so the schools can help them. High-school students can be matched with seniors to offer help with driving, running errands, yard work, and so on.

Schools and retirees are a custom-made match, but in Wynott, ALL hands are called upon to volunteer, and all structures and systems within the community can stand to benefit from the extra help.

5

HOW WE PAY FOR STUFF

WHY KEEP FEEDING THE TAPEWORM?

When the whole world is your market, the corner shop—if it's still open for business—seems pretty pedestrian. How are you gonna keep them down on the farm after they've eaten cheap New Zealand strawberries from Wal-Mart in January?

All of those quaint bumper stickers with warm fuzzy thoughts about sustainability and buying locally just don't seem to be resonating.

WELCOME TO WYNOTT

To get a better sense of the situation, next time you spend money in a big-box chain store or a corporate chain restaurant, think about tapeworms, because that's how they operate in a small community.

The only goal of a tapeworm is uncontrolled growth. It enjoys your warm hospitality by attaching itself to your digestive tract and absorbing as many nutrients as it can get. When you eat a strawberry, you don't get the benefit of those vitamins and calories, the tapeworm does. When you spend money in a national chain, the profits go to the stockholders, who are not likely to live in your neighborhood. The local people employed by the store receive as little in pay and benefits as possible. The merchandise is probably not produced in your town, your state, or even your nation, but wherever it is produced, the people doing that work are also receiving as little in pay and benefits as possible.

Very little of the money your community spends in the chain store or restaurant is re-circulated within your community. Most of it is hustled out and gobbled up to fuel the tapeworm's unlimited growth. A corporate franchise will take as much as it can from your community and invest only as much as is necessary to maintain a customer base. To do anything else would be to deprive its shareholders of profits, which goes against a corporation's primary purpose: to maximize shareholder value. If not, it's not a corporation; it's

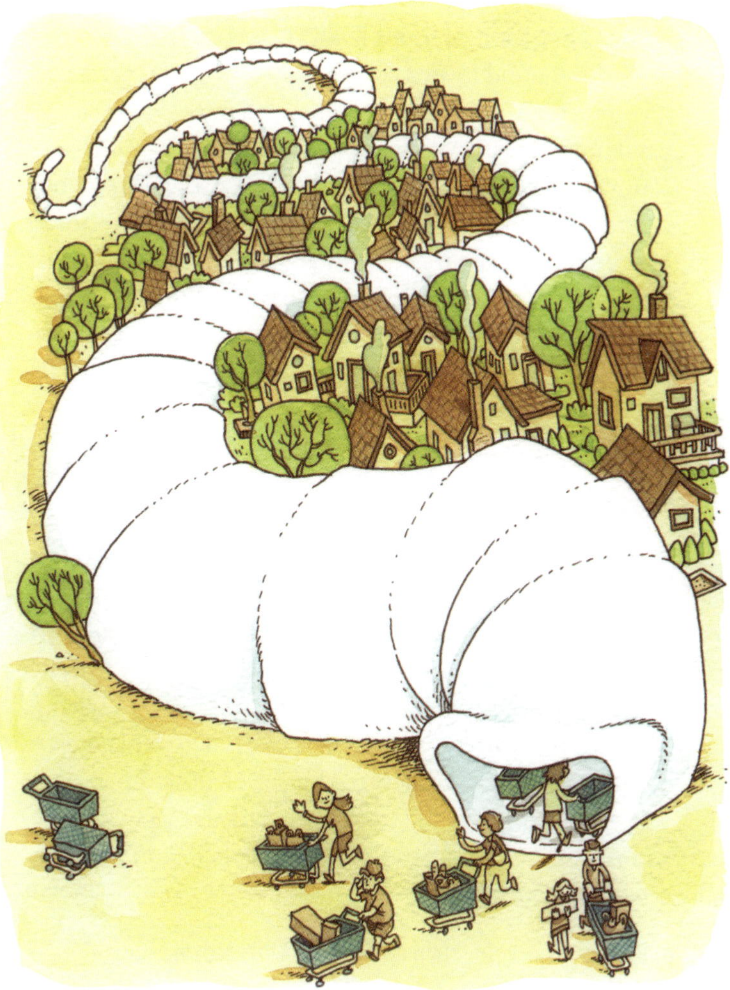

some other kind of organization. A corporation is not, by nature, good or evil. It is simply always hungry.

Nothing happens in this universe without an exchange of energy. No life form can function for very long without this steady give and take, including your community. Money is nothing more than a symbol of energy being exchanged. When the money leaves your community, your community loses energy, and eventually your community will not be able to support life. Which makes it a pretty pointless place to live.

So what to do?

WYNOTT PRINT YOUR OWN MONEY?

You don't have to be anti-business to be pro-community. You just have to let business know that your community means business. Local business. Locally owned businesses keep more money circulating within their community, and this circulation is what keeps a community vital, energized, and healthy. One great way to keep the money working locally is by developing a community currency that's only good *within certain geographic boundaries.*

In Wynott you can earn and spend Wy-Notes.

Imagine that you could earn the equivalent of ten dollars for every hour you spent helping out in a

VOLUNTEERING
OUTDOOR WORK
COMMUNITY EDUCATION
10
10
10
10
WY-NOTE
STORE
DONA-TIONS
BUY SERVICES
SUPPORT THE COMMUNITY
PURCHASE GOODS

classroom at your local grade school or raking leaves for your elderly neighbors. If you put in five hours, you've got fifty Wy-Notes to spend around town. On Friday night, you take your sweetheart to the movies, and afterwards you hit the local café for a late-night slice of pie. Not only did you help out worthy causes and support local businesses, but you just got a night out on the town for doing something you otherwise might have done for free. And if you would have otherwise done all of that volunteer work for free, how much more might you do if it means hot dates and pie? And how many people who wouldn't otherwise find the time to volunteer might suddenly make room in their schedule to earn some Wy-Notes?

Wy-Notes don't replace federal currency. They simply work in tandem with dollars to strengthen the local economy. Because there's no benefit to saving or hoarding Wy-Notes, they circulate faster. More transactions and more connections make a Wynott community more resilient and energetic. A community currency encourages people to buy locally, which also means that they don't travel as far.

An important role of Wy-Notes is as a stimulus to expand volunteerism. Getting people to collaborate is always easier when there's some benefit to them. But it's more than compensation. In Wynott, rewarding people for excellence is always the goal. People who serve are acknowledged and appreciated, and Wy-Notes are a concrete expression of appreciation for a job well done.

In Wynott, Wy-Notes are granted to organizations that need volunteers, like schools and nonprofits. Interest-free Wy-Note loans are given to promote local entrepreneurship, helping to create jobs and start new businesses. Any business or individual can list their services in the Wy-Note directory for a small membership fee that covers the cost of administration. Wy-Notes can also be an incentive for homeless people who are able and willing to work.

Take a moment to list all of the skills you possess that you'd be willing to offer in exchange for Wy-Notes. You could have the kind of job that puts you in demand—maybe you cut hair or fix cars. Or you might not have the kind of job that is easily translated into Wy-Notes—maybe you are a project manager with a wonky and specific skill set that doesn't make sense outside of your office building. But maybe you also happen to be able to play and teach guitar, and install software, and dog-sit. With Wy-Notes, instead of crashing in front of the TV after work every day, you can find ways to make yourself more available to the community while earning a currency that you will spread further around the community.

Wy-Notes can also be used to compensate (in full or in part) people outside of Wynott who are recruited for projects that might otherwise be a pro bono service due to budget constraints. Imagine building a new dog run in a local park. An offer of Wy-Notes may make it easier to bring in an experienced designer.

Community currency is an easy concept to grasp if you've ever been in a casino. When you walk around with a bucket of tokens, you're going to spend them in the casino—maybe on blackjack, maybe at the roulette wheel, maybe at the buffet—but there they will stay. And you're not going to take that bucketful of tokens and hoard it in a mattress somewhere—you're going to unload. Casinos know this and count on it. Of course, you can always cash in your chips. They have a solid monetary value that connects them to the real world. But if you've got just one token in your hand, are you going to stand in line at the cashier and exchange it, or are you going to slip it into the closest slot machine?

> **Community currency is an easy concept to grasp if you've ever been in a casino.**

You probably don't want to turn your community into a casino, but we could learn a thing or two from their prosperity. Casinos know how to keep the action rolling, and one of the secrets of their success is community currency.

Community currency, similar to but not the same as bartering, is an old concept that has meant different things in different places at different times. In the Great Depression, various local "stamp scrips" made it possible for a lot of Americans to stay fed and stay afloat during a period of scarce resources, low employment, and limited imports.

Community currency is now in use in over 2,500 cities nationwide, including more than seventy-five U.S. communities. In Berkshires, Massachusetts, residents can spend locally minted "Berkshares" in more than 360 local businesses offering everything from entertainment to health care to legal counsel to auto repair to mortuary services. Five local banks handle Berkshares and will exchange them for dollars.

One of the oldest and largest community currencies is the Ithaca, New York, "Hours" system, where one Hour is equal to ten dollars. Many other regions have followed their lead, using an Hour exchange that makes it possible for community members to exchange time and services. According to the Hour Exchange of Portland, Maine, "If you give an hour of your time helping someone, providing a service, then you can receive an hour of someone else's time who provides a service you need. Time is what our members exchange. We are a community currency based on time. We believe all people are created equal, and so is our time."

You don't have to boycott all corporate franchises, goods, and services in order to support your local community. Patronizing local business doesn't make you anti-corporate. After all, in a global economy, any entrepreneur who starts a small business from his or

WELCOME TO WYNOTT

her garage has the potential to expand into a worldwide operation, and if that were you, or your neighbor, you'd be glad to have been a part of that success. It's also true progress to live in an age of ready access to goods and services from around the world. Life would be pretty hard without coffee, which can't be grown in the continental United States!

But there are a lot of factors in play that make all that possible, and one small glitch can throw everything into chaos. A 2010 volcano eruption in Iceland, for instance, shut down air travel and impacted trade across all of Europe, revealing how vulnerable an international trade system really is. A tsunami that devastated Japan sent economic ripples across the world: The lack of just one Japan-made electronic component meant that a U.S. auto factory idled workers, halting production, and car dealers nationwide had empty spaces on their lots.

When disaster strikes, it's good to know that you can rely on the people around you. One of the greatest potentials of Wy-Notes IS the untapped potential of the people who exchange these denominations. A community currency ferrets out the underutilized talents, skills, and knowledge of people who are suddenly very creative with how they're willing to spend or accept this local money.

6

How We Get Around

WHY DO WE SETTLE FOR FIVE MILES PER HOUR?

Five miles per hour. That's the formula of cost-to-benefit for the average American car, according to Ivan Illich's *Energy and Equity*. Depending on what you drive, you're spending, on average, somewhere between $3,000 and $13,000 per year to own and operate a motor vehicle. Combine hours spent in traffic with the vehicle price, then factor in taxes, fuel, maintenance, repairs, financing, and depreciation—not counting parking costs and traffic tickets—and it becomes apparent that

WELCOME TO WYNOTT

instead of your car working to serve you, you are working to serve your car.

Cars are expensive and time-consuming. It's no secret that they pollute our environment. They also affect our mental health. Consider the increase in congestion and the rise of road rage incidents. A daily commute can cause stress, anxiety, and even depression. And cars are dangerous, killing forty thousand people a year in this nation. That means that since 1900, the number of Americans who have died in car crashes is more than double the number of Americans killed in every war, combined. And we're not really improving our statistics. Seatbelts and airbags can only do so much for the modern drivers who check Twitter, apply mascara, and slurp hot beverages while maneuvering through rush-hour traffic.

HOW WE GET AROUND

The dysfunction of our society is best illustrated by the stressed-out, overworked, and out-of-shape person who spends forty-five minutes driving from the office to the gym, fights for the parking spot closest to the door, then squeezes in a short workout on the stair climber before driving home and collapsing into bed, exhausted, wondering where the day went.

Commuting is brutal. From a dollars-and-cents perspective, gas, mileage, and wear and tear on a car can all be factored. These are substantial costs. But what about the minutes of a person's life? The hours? What kind of wear and tear does a person sustain by sitting in rush-hour traffic every day? If you wake up at six and hit the sack by ten, you've got sixteen waking hours in your day. If it takes you forty-five minutes to get to work and another forty-five to get back home, that's over ten percent of your day spent in traffic. Ten percent of your day! You could put all of those minutes together and get that commute done all at once by sitting in your car for a bit over sixteen days and nights, straight. You probably don't have (or can't take) sixteen days of vacation. But if you cut your commute down to ten minutes by locating closer to your work, it would be like giving yourself a free twelve-day

> You could put all of those minutes together and get that commute done all at once by sitting in your car for a bit over sixteen days and nights, straight.

vacation every year. Or if you're the workaholic type, that's twelve days wasted when you could have been making more money. Over a career of forty years, that forty-five-minute commute adds up to 650 days. That's almost two years of your life spent in rush-hour traffic. But somehow it feels like more, doesn't it?

The number of cars on the road has naturally grown with the increase in population. But the number of cars per capita has also grown. Although our households now have fewer family members, we own more cars. There was a time when the family car was the only car. Everyone in the house shared one vehicle and made it work, just like the famous opening carpool scene of *The Jetsons*. But that cartoon got the future wrong. Not only do we not have robot house cleaners, our traffic is worse than ever.

> **Not only do we not have robot house cleaners, our traffic is worse than ever.**

There was a time when it was okay to hitchhike or to pick up a hitchhiker. It just made sense, if you were heading in that direction, to join forces with someone else doing the same. Unfortunately, the jerks of the world made hitchhiking a risky endeavor, and Hollywood screenwriters ruined it further by making it the plotline of too many horror films. So don't hitchhike. This book does not endorse hitchhiking and will not be held liable for unwitting travelers who climb into cars with psycho killers. This book does, however, encourage you to develop your own trustworthy hitchhiking network.

WYNOTT SHARE THE ROAD AND LIGHTEN THE LOAD?

In the words of comedian Steven Wright, "Everywhere is walking distance if you have the time." And that perfectly sums up Wynott. In this pedestrian-centric town, walking is always the first choice because it's healthy, safe, and pleasant. And there are so many great places to walk to that people are always out milling about. But walking isn't the only way to get from Point A to Point B. Bikes and public transportation are also attractive options, and these modes of transport are supported and encouraged.

And when all else fails—there's still the automobile. Preferably a full automobile, maximizing the mileage and the legroom. This is where your hitchhiking network comes in. Going to the office? Hop in with a coworker. Heading to the grocery store? Offer a lift to a neighbor who needs a few staples. Share rides with friends and streamline errands and outings within your family. You'll save time, mileage, and money, and you'll gain camaraderie and crackerjack navigational abilities. You'll feel good about being part of the traffic solution instead of the traffic problem. All of it increases the quality of your own life as well as the desirability of Wynott.

It's easy enough to get into the habit of sharing rides informally. But Wynott also happens to be the hub of a car-sharing service.

A car-sharing service is simply a fleet of cars shared by a group of members who rent a vehicle as needed, by the hour or by the day. These services have been operating for many years in densely populated cities where public transportation is the norm and a car is really only needed for out-of-town trips, moving large items, or special occasions.

Car-sharing has recently blossomed near universities, where students are in no position to afford the payments, maintenance, parking, and insurance costs of a car they only rarely need to use. This new generation appreciates the savings and convenience of shared vehicles and is helping to move the concept beyond the college campus. Now budget-minded families, savvy singles, and forward-thinking businesses are taking advantage of this idea.

Car-sharing services are popping up in cities all over the world, with names like Hour Car, Zipcar, and I-Go. The British call it a "car club"; in other places the service is known as *autodelen* (Netherlands), *autopartage* (France), *bildeling* (Denmark), *auto condivisa* (Italy), and *bilpool* (Sweden).

HOW WE GET AROUND

In a place like Wynott, where walking, biking, and public transit are attractive ways to get around, a car-sharing service can do a brisk business. The way it works is, cars are kept at a variety of locations, known as parking "pods." These pods are easily accessible by public transportation. Members make reservations by phone, computer, or text, and once they are confirmed, a car will be waiting for them at the appointed pod.

Another way to get around is to take a look at our inactive public vehicles. The average school bus is only used for a few hours a day, five days a week. When it's not moving kids to and from schools or fieldtrips, it can be put to use as the Wynott Circulator. A volunteer driver can circulate through the neighborhood in a yellow school bus twice a day to get people to the shopping district, the grocery store, the clinics, the parks, and so on.

People would be glad to spend a buck or two, or a Wy-Note or two, to know that every Wednesday they can catch a school bus on the corner and ride it to the grocery store and back. Or every Saturday they can catch a school bus on the corner and ride it to the library and back. This not only cuts down traffic and pollution in Wynott, it also gives more options to seniors, to families with one car, and to people who can't drive or who choose to drive less. The Wynott Circulator could run for a very small charge and could even make a profit to help offset local school transportation costs.

8:30am
SCHOOL BUS
Elementary School
SCHOOL BUS
WYNOTT CIRCULAR
WYNOTT CIRCULAR
12:45pm

HOW WE GET AROUND

WHY DO WE HAVE LEGS WHEN WE NEVER USE THEM?

The United States has the world's highest obesity rate, and we have nearly the highest rate of car ownership—one car for every 2.09 people. Not 2.09 licensed drivers, but 2.09 *people,* meaning babies and children, prisoners, shut-ins—everybody. Is it possible that we are all overweight because the average American only walks three hundred yards *per day*?

We are a car culture. Henry Ford got us started, with easy credit that made it possible for the average working man to own the machine that had, until then, been accessible only to the upper crust. Automobiles went from luxury to necessity for the millions of Americans who had moved to the suburbs, far from their jobs and away from public transportation. Gas prices were low, demand for cars was high, and by 1960, more than three out of four American families owned at least one car.

As Americans spent more and more time on the road, the love affair became a committed marriage. Commuting meant driving. Every errand demanded a trip in the car. From Chuck Berry to the Beach Boys, it seemed like every other song on the radio was an anthem to the automobile. Drive-in movies entertained without the inconvenience of getting out of the car. Drive-through restaurants trumpeted the novelty of meals served window-to-window. It could even be argued that a percentage of the population was conceived in the back seats of those roomy American automobiles.

Streetcars were quickly dismantled as America transitioned to an automobile economy. Living in the city once meant that you could walk to a nearby corner store and get most of the things you needed. If it wasn't on the corner, a streetcar would soon come by, and you could ride downtown to get whatever else you needed. This system disappeared as supermarkets came into existence. Why walk to the corner pharmacy, grocer, butcher, or baker when you could drive to a supermarket and get everything under one roof? Built with ample parking spaces on busy streets, this convenient option was not really optional once the corner shops had been driven out by the supermarkets and the shopping malls.

The fact that the American shopping mall owes its popularity and success to the automobile is an odd piece of irony.

Planned by Victor Gruen for Edina, Minnesota, the first indoor shopping mall in the United States was only one element of a much larger development plan that included apartment buildings, medical facilities, houses, schools, a lake, and a park. Gruen modeled the mall after the downtown arcades of his native Austria. All the great European cities boasted these central gathering places where community members could eat, drink, and visit. In this tradition, Gruen furnished his mall with artwork, fountains, flowers, and decorative lighting to foster an atmosphere of intimacy, excitement, and leisure. He included wide central spaces for community gatherings. Gruen did not want a suburban alternative to nearby downtown Minneapolis; he felt he was building from scratch the American downtown as it should be.

But the new downtown was not built—only the shopping mall was completed. Dayton Company developed Southdale Center for $20 million in 1954. Department stores Dayton's and Donaldson's joined Woolworth's and Walgreen's Pharmacy as anchor stores. Smaller shops and eateries filled in.

The concept took off like a rocket. Cornfields across America sprouted these new shopping meccas. Although Gruen was a socialist who despised the American suburban lifestyle of the 1950s, he unwittingly fathered the iconic focal point of suburban American capitalism.

While it did succeed in attracting people, the new American shopping mall had a very different vibe than Gruen's inspiration, the European mall. In Europe, a mall is commonly recognized as an exclusively pedestrian avenue, lined with shops and cafes and shaded by trees. Integrated into their surrounding neighborhoods, these malls are easily accessed by foot. Nobody walked to Southdale—nobody lived within walking distance. Instead, shoppers parked their cars in one of the 5,272 parking spaces. When they entered the mall they were guided by the inward-facing design of the controlled environment to roam in a circle and shop.

American malls are islands unto themselves, awash in a sea of parked cars. They are located on major traffic arterials, which can be quite hostile to the few brave shoppers making their way in on foot, pushing strollers, or pedaling bikes. This was not only a departure from the tree-lined European mall, but also from the typical American shopping district—rows of downtown shops that faced sidewalks, handy by foot or streetcar. As the shoppers got into cars and drove their spending money out to the suburbs, stores went dark downtown and all along the main streetcar lines. Daily errands could no longer be easily achieved as a pedestrian. We now live our lives through, for, and within our cars. At first, it was fun and sexy. But the honeymoon is over.

HOW WE GET AROUND

Oil is in limited supply, and the price will only go up. Detroit, "Motor City," the once-glorious world capital of car manufacturing, is working to reinvent itself. Pollution and congestion are serious concerns. We're running out of parking spaces. Our streets, once the shared spaces of our neighborhoods, have become the exclusive domain of high-speed vehicles, and it's every squirrel, cat, dog, jogger, and school kid for him- or herself.

> It's every squirrel, cat, dog, jogger, and school kid for him- or herself.

Each morning we enter our attached garages, climb into our climate-controlled automobiles, press the garage-door button, and head to work. We isolate ourselves from our fellow commuters by listening to the radio, chatting on the phone, or even watching tiny screens. The stress of traffic creates a me-against-the-world attitude. Road rage and fender-benders are the hallmark of every rush hour, every morning and every evening, on every route, in every city. We're disconnected, and we're in danger.

And we're out of shape, overweight, and tired. The solution is so simple: Go for a walk.

American cities were once built around pedestrians. Streetcars traveled seven miles per hour down roadways that shared space with bikers, walkers, horses, and the occasional truck or automobile. Storefronts were in the front, not set back behind forty rows of asphalt parking spaces. The built environment was built for people, not for machines.

It could happen again.

Close your eyes for a moment and imagine yourself in Times Square, New York City. Do you see lots of people heading in all different directions? How about all of the flashing lights and neon signs? Okay, now can you hear the honking, smell the exhaust fumes, see the rows and rows of cars and taxis? No you can't! Because Times Square, one of the busiest acres of land in the known world, has been converted into a pedestrian zone. Traffic has been blocked from 42nd to 47th Streets and has been replaced by new shops and pedestrian plazas. If walkers can make it there, they can make it anywhere. New York has the highest pedestrian density in America. Despite—or because of—its heavy traffic, a huge percentage of New Yorkers prefer to hoof it. In the Big Apple, where 6 percent of the racing rats walk to work, the pedestrian danger index is a low 28.

The Pedestrian Danger Index was created by Transportation for America to rank all U.S. cities with populations over one million. It is calculated by dividing the average pedestrian fatality rate by the percentage of residents walking to work. Cities currently score between zero and 221.

So where is the worst place to walk? For some strange reason, the top four cities for pedestrian traffic deaths are all located in the Sunshine State. You'd think that it would be easier to see where you're going with the top down, but those friendly Florida drivers run over a lot of little old ladies who are trying to cross the street. Researchers have many theories on why this is so, but the main reason cited is the torrid pace of development in Florida: seven times faster than any other state, from 1950 until present. Rapid development has prioritized roadways designed and built to accommodate a lot of traffic and to move it with the utmost speed and efficiency. Traffic meaning cars, not feet.

Fast-growing metropolitan areas, mostly in warm climates, turn out to be the least safe for people on foot. It might seem that pedestrians are killed more often just because the warmer climate means that people are out and about more. Not so. Consider the fact that 1.3 percent of Kissimmee, Florida, residents walk to work, and in chilly Minneapolis, Minnesota, a hearty 2.4 percent of residents walk to work. The Minneapolis pedestrian danger index is a mere 22; Kissimmee's is 221. Nationwide, more people walk to work in Ithaca, New York, than in any other city. Their pedestrian danger index? Six. So weather is no excuse. For every day that's too hot for walking in Kissimmee, there's a corresponding day that's too cold for walking in Ithaca.

When you start to compare city obesity rankings with their pedestrian danger indexes, a pattern emerges. The places least friendly to walkers are often home to the most overweight. It's not about the weather; it's about the built environment. Hot weather can't make you fat. Cities that were built to accommodate cars and not pedestrians *can* make you fat. And if you try to get outside and run off those extra pounds, you just might get run over.

Cities that were built to accommodate cars and not pedestrians *can* make you fat.

What to do?

HOW WE GET AROUND

WYNOTT TAKE BACK THE STREETS?

There is much to be learned, in the United States and around the world.

In Wynott, residential streets take a tip from Amsterdam, where a funny-sounding concept called *woonerf* is making it possible for people to get the most out of their streets. These living thoroughfares blur the lines between road and sidewalk, deliberately doing away with delineated curbs and boulevards. They can be found in most European cities, and in New Zealand, Australia, and Hong Kong. The pedestrian mall is a concept familiar to some U.S. cities, and the *woonerf* is now slowly working its way into the car-loving U.S. lexicon.

So what the heck is a *woonerf*?

Think of your street like a timeshare. At certain times, it's most needed by cars. But when the workday and the workweek is over, it can make a great place to bike or to play a game of catch or street hockey. Many neighborhoods get a small taste of this once a year during an annual block party, when they close off a street and have a gathering. It's a liberating feeling of community, and makes the block seem more spacious, not to mention much safer.

Woonerfs create block parties every day, either by restricting auto traffic to certain hours or by limiting the flow of auto traffic and giving precedence to pedestrians and cyclists. Most side streets in Tokyo

a.m.

p.m.

organically operate, without mandate, on the *woonerf* principle. In the United Kingdom, "home zones" are residential streets that do the same thing, incorporating traffic-calming features that cars must navigate, preventing them from picking up speed in a straight line.

During certain hours, a *woonerf* can close a street or alley and create a common space. These common spaces can be home to lovely landscaped areas, created and maintained by volunteers. They can hold play areas, social gatherings, even performances from time to time.

But it doesn't have to stop there. Why not close off sections of some streets for good? There are so many blocks of street that could be permanently closed off and never missed, especially those short city blocks that often run east–west. A gate could be installed to make it accessible strictly to sanitation workers, street sweepers, snowplows, and the like, as needed.

If every other short block in a section of your neighborhood were closed, so that there were only one way in and out of an alley, it would restrict alley traffic to only the people who lived there, saving wear and tear on the road and making it safer for kids on bikes and less vulnerable to vandals and thieves.

If blocks were closed off to auto traffic in a sensible pattern throughout a neighborhood, it would vastly reduce speed and significantly cut down on unnecessary through traffic. Certain blocks could be permanently closed. Or the pattern could rotate. Imagine if the street in front of your house was closed off each Tuesday for the length of your block and that the street behind it was closed each Wednesday. You'd adapt to the schedule quickly, but people who didn't live nearby would never bother cutting through your neighborhood—too confusing. The only traffic would be residents or people with a reason to visit. Not only would residents come to appreciate it, but it would undoubtedly have a positive impact on property values.

In new developments, *woonerfs* could be built in from the start, enabling a more efficient use of space and smaller yards. This is particularly helpful to maximize land for infill developments in the city, constrained by existing construction.

Woonerfs . . . Wynott?

WHY LIVE HERE IF YOU NEVER LEAVE YOUR HOUSE?

It's too cold. It's too hot. The streets are dead. The streets are too crowded. I don't want to run into anybody I know. I don't know anybody.

We Americans have quarantined ourselves into our living rooms and left our TVs in charge. We are only motivated to move if it means spending money we don't have on stuff we don't need because that's what the TV told us to do. Or the computer. Or the smartphone.

What we're supposed to do is get comfortable, relax, take a break. Because we're worth it. This means we don't want to get cold in the winter or hot in the summer. We like our climate control. We like our remotes. When summer comes, we'll go out for a little while, get a little sunshine—but only if it's not too much of a hassle, not too inconvenient. Not *too* sunny . . . .

We want our kids to get exercise, so we sign them up for some organized activities and spend a lot of time driving back and forth to those. When there's time, we let them play in the yard, where we can keep an eye on them. But only for ten minutes—because otherwise they'll get sunburned, or bit by something, or kidnapped. It's just not safe out there.

Even as our scientific advances bring radical improvements to health care, we have created a new disease that has reached a national epidemic in our children: Nature Deficit Disorder, or NDD. Defined by Richard Louv in his book *Last Child in the Woods,* NDD is thought to be the cause of a wide range of behavioral problems in kids who never get to go out and explore. Sensational stories on a twenty-four-hour news feed have made parents fearful of allowing their children to go anywhere or do anything other than sit in front of a screen—the same screen that's the source of these sensational news stories.

There is a disproportionately high number of negative news items compared to positive items. You'll see umpteen stabbings for every one neighbor-does-good-deed feature. Not because nobody ever does anything good, but because it doesn't keep us on the edge of our seats like the bad news does. The news builds its ratings by feeding into the drama of Us versus Them. You just can't watch the ten o'clock news without focusing on your enemies—the criminals, of course, lots of criminals. But also the sports teams who are trying to take your team down. The politicians who you didn't vote for and wouldn't vote for, and all of their followers, who just make you sick to your stomach. Plus all of those health hazards and medical malfunctions that are actively trying to give you cancer. You could change the title of nearly any news program to "Who's Out to Get You."

We feel it our duty to stay in front of the TV and be informed—OR ELSE! Or else we might be poisoned or murdered or scammed. We're afraid to go out because we might get swine flu or bird flu or poodle flu. We might get kidnapped, carjacked, or bushwhacked.

Might.

What we *will* get for sure, if we stay on our butts in front of the TV, is inertia, obesity, stress, and anxiety. "Information anxiety" to be precise. Also known as "information overload" and "information fatigue." These terms have all been coined to describe the very real phenomenon of what happens when we are constantly barraged with news. Richard Saul Wurman explains, in his book *Information Anxiety,* that a weekday edition of the *New York Times* contains more information than the average person was likely to come across in an entire *lifetime* in seventeenth-century England. It's theorized that humans have a hundred-mile news radius capacity. Anything farther away than that is too abstract to comprehend and therefore not relevant to our daily lives.

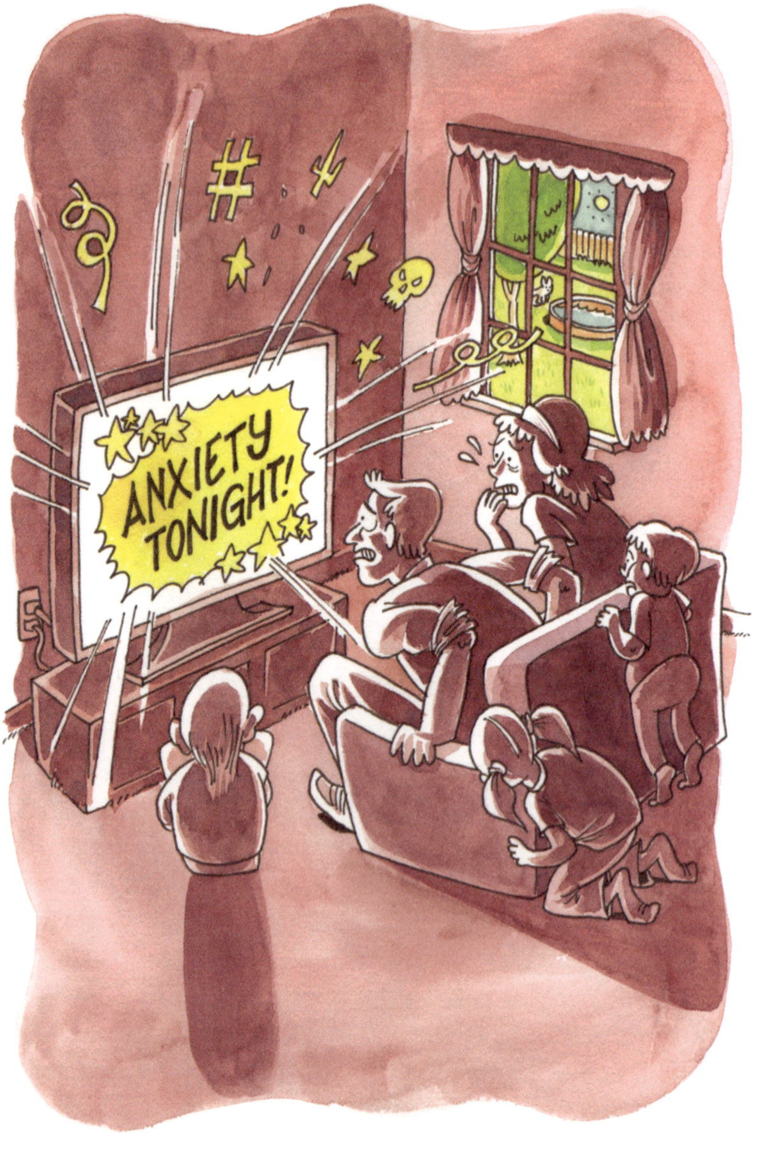
ANXIETY TONIGHT!

HOW WE GET AROUND

In a global economy, of course, we are more and more connected to world events, and a tsunami in a distant land could very well impact our own retirement funds. But there's too much news. Our brains have not yet evolved to the point where we can adequately process the nonstop information that daily comes our way. We've got four-cylinder brains and we're trying to run on eight. We can't keep track of it all. We seek to be enlightened, but what we are is entrenched and encumbered.

Despite the fact that most Americans are relatively safe, healthy, and satisfied, numerous opinion polls indicate that we live with a level of fear that far exceeds our actual risk of physical, mental, or financial danger. With all of the commotion and distraction, we're living in our perception instead of our reality.

The negative news that we absorb—and yes, the bulk of the news is negative or sensational—causes us to fear and distrust the people around us. It's like when you hear about a case of head lice and your own scalp immediately starts itching.

> ... we're just locking ourselves in with all of the creeps, brutes, perverts, and swindlers ...

We are paralyzed by our perceptions—it's too dangerous out there. We think we're safest at home in front of the TV, where it's cozy and warm, but really, we're just locking ourselves in with all of the creeps, brutes, perverts, and swindlers who make the headlines on our screens and then get inside of our heads and live there.

What we really need to fear is fear itself. And we should be very afraid of fear, because *fear* is making our world less safe. By keeping cautious, law-abiding people off the streets and disconnected from each other, fear encourages people not to look out for each other.

The world isn't any worse than it was when the Vikings were out marauding and pillaging. Or when the black plague was wiping out villages, or when polio was closing down swimming pools. If you are a living creature, there's always an element of danger. A meteor could take us all out any day now, and there's just nothing to be done about that. So stop worrying. Enough with the self-imposed quarantine—click off the TV. Put down the paper. Turn down the radio. Log off the computer. Go see for yourself what it's really like outside.

WYNOTT GET OUT AND GET SOME AIR?

This may sound completely radical, but you don't actually have to watch the news. Don't believe it? Try going on a news fast and avoid watching, hearing, and reading it for a week, or a month, or longer, and see how much better your outlook is. Plus, you won't be exposed to all of those hideous commercials that build false desires for junk you don't need, not to mention the political ads that make you want to move to the North Pole.

If there's some critically important piece of information, or if you are in imminent danger, someone will tell you. Someone is always willing to tell you bad news. But very little of the news is stuff you actually need to know. If you have just a little bit of common sense, you can avoid most dangerous situations. And as for the rest of the dangerous situations, well, did watching the news help them? Stuff happens. Don't waste time worrying about it—worry is the solution to nothing.

Fresh air is the solution to just about everything. Getting your butt out there and being part of nature makes nature part of you. Being part of the community makes the community part of you. So go mingle. It's nice out. A few snowflakes aren't going to kill you.

Winter City/Summer City

Wynott is a community where people mingle and linger, a community that people want to inhabit, want to support. Whatever the climate, it's okay to go outside, most of the time.

In Wynott, people are out and about all year round. No matter how far north it is, Wynott is not a winter city that shuts down for three to six months out of the year. Certainly, there are bad-weather days, but they number around thirty, not half of a year. There's really no such thing as a winter city. That idea is pure myth, a mind game, a figment of the imagination and an excuse to be sedentary. Some of the world's greatest cities would not exist if this were true.

In Wynott, winter is treated the same as it is in Copenhagen, or Toronto, or Beijing. There are outdoor markets to explore, outdoor cafes to patronize, outdoor arts events to attend, and outdoor activities to take part in. Marathons, loppets, and walking clubs keep people active. Many hearty souls are even out on bikes. Vendors sell hot coffee, mulled wine, roasted nuts, and other toasty treats. Heat lamps and blankets are plentiful for outdoor seating and mingling. Strung lights make the atmosphere festive as the days grow shorter.

And Wynott can be hot. However close to the equator, Wynott offers reasons for people to be outside: cooling activities, shady oases, refreshing fare to eat and drink, places to see and be seen.

When there are interesting things to do and see, people will come, and more than anything, people attract people. Engaged citizens discourage riffraff from taking over. More people out on the streets make the streets safer and the city more livable. More foot traffic is good for local businesses and community. Fresh air and camaraderie are good for the people.

Serious crime is also less common in Wynott because an engaged and active citizenry just makes it harder for the riffraff to get away with very much.

Extrapolating from the "safety-in-numbers" adage—when people are connected, when neighbors are involved in their neighborhoods, when the streets are full of pedestrians—the good guys simply outnumber the bad guys, and it's tough for gangs and creeps to wield significant power.

Peace officers in Wynott put the emphasis on peace. While a more visible police presence has been shown to cut down petty crimes in public places, it doesn't make crime disappear, it just makes crime relocate. Wynott is a friendly place, but it's really inhospitable to criminals. They're the only ones who don't get the chance to grow and thrive. And we're okay with that.

7

Where We Live

WHY ARE WE STUCK IN THE FIFTIES?

The American household has changed quite a bit since the 1950s. Nearly 90 percent of households in 1950 were made up of families with one mom, one dad, a gaggle of kids, and often one or two grandparents. Not only are families now smaller, but there are fewer of them. The 2010 Census has that number down under 70 percent. The fastest-growing household type of the last fifty years has been the single-member household. Across the board, in all adult age groups, more and more people live alone. Since 1950, the number of single-member households has nearly tripled.

The U.S. Census clearly shows our changing demographic. Behind the hard data and pie charts, so many factors have come into play . . . everything from the much lower cost of air travel to the widespread use of birth control to the cultural revolution of the 1960s to advances in modern medicine. Today, senior citizens live longer, but they rarely live with their families. Women have fewer babies, they have them later in life, and they may or may not live with the father of their children. Nuclear families tend to be smaller. Singles are single longer. Marrieds are married more often. Stepfamilies are more common. Extended families are spread across the nation as members cross state lines for college, job opportunities, and warm-weather retirement dreams. We are mobile. We are restless. We don't like sharing bathrooms. And we don't have to. The United States now has more private housing square footage per capita than any other nation in the world.

From an urban planning perspective, there are downsides and upsides to our new social reality. For generations, the American Dream has been to own a nice house, raise a big family in it, and stay there until they carry you out feet first. This means that a lot of big houses, ideal for the pitter-patter of many little feet, will spend years hosting only the shuffle-shuffle of one or two senior citizens. The housing stock isn't turning over fast enough to accommodate upcoming families.

It is acceptable that as the size of a family contracts and expands, one house gets traded in for another. BUT downsizing doesn't always mean what it used to. Smaller households are living in larger houses, expecting more amenities, and stretching out to fill more square footage. We need to start actively encouraging housing turnover whenever possible and appropriate, because otherwise we're looking at some serious large-scale inefficiency, the fallout from which we're only just starting to see.

Reality has changed, demographics have changed, and the population density has changed. All of this has had an effect on the built environment. Although there are more people on Earth than ever before, here in the United States we're still spreading farther out, in search of more elbow room than our grandparents needed.

Today, the choice to buy a house in the suburbs is generally motivated by a better square-footage-per-dollar ratio. Expectations have dramatically changed from the postwar generation who thought nothing of raising six kids in a house with one bathroom. Although people are having fewer children and having them later in life, they want bigger kitchens, bigger closets, bigger garages, more bathrooms, family rooms, mud rooms, craft rooms, and media rooms. The farther out they go, the bigger the house they can get in a neighborhood they deem to be "better." Not to mention newer. As one boom-time Las Vegas homebuyer disdainfully explains in journalist Daniel McGinn's book *House Lust,* living in a used home means living in "other people's ick." Heading farther out means paying less money for more square footage. But these buyers don't pay the real costs that go into making that new exurban development possible—the infrastructure, the road maintenance, the new water lines. The devaluation of existing housing stock.

A city like Minneapolis, which once housed 500,000 to 600,000 people, now holds only 382,000, even as its greater metropolitan area (including its twin city, St. Paul) sprawls outward to an impressive mass of 341 square miles. This puts the Twin Cities at number ten on the U.S. Census's list of 100 U.S. Urbanized Areas Ranked by Square Miles of Sprawl. Without any of the geographic barriers that some cities face, like mountains or oceans, Midwestern areas like the Twin Cities are free to just spill outward, seemingly unto infinity.

So what's wrong with that? In a free-market society, builders must be allowed to take a gamble on a new development and see if they can sell their wares. Homebuyers must have the freedom to live where they choose.

But every time a new home is built farther out, it creates a domino effect. One household vacates, another takes its place, another takes its place, and at some point, there's a house somewhere that is vacant, and nobody wants to move into it. What we've got right now is an economy where there are too many sellers and not enough buyers. More and more people are in the position where they can't buy until they sell what they've already got. But we're still building new suburbs farther out, which means we're expanding our obligation to erect and to maintain more and more infrastructure.

In the entire Twin Cities metropolitan area, to continue with our example, we've got 3.8 million bedrooms and only 2.8 million people. That makes it tough for the city to take care of the parks, streets, and schools when there's a shrinking tax base with a decreasing ability to pay for services. Schools that were once bursting with kids have been forced to close down due to decreasing enrollment—not because there are fewer kids, but because they're spread too far around.

Once a school is built, it can't move. But the citizens can move out from around it. Since we can't move the building, we have to move the kids, and we're busing in zigzag patterns during rush hour going every which way. That's more vehicles on the road, paid for by taxpayers, polluting and clogging up traffic, eating up the time in children's days.

Why do we continue to sprawl, when our existing housing stock is underutilized?

When we just blow with the wind and let the free market shape our housing choices, we waste a lot of money in the long run, as taxpayers, as homeowners, and as renters. By not considering the impact of our moves, we participate in school closings, traffic jams, loss of farm and forestland, urban decay, and more. But how should we know all of this? We're just trying to find something we can afford in a place where we feel like we belong.

> We're just trying to find something we can afford in a place where we feel like we belong.

And we're not getting much help from our real estate agents.

The way our real estate system is set up, the agent is not motivated, encouraged, or in most cases, *allowed* to factor in the most appropriate option for both buyer and seller and give true guidance and expertise. There's no incentive to go the extra mile to find the best fit for a family, for a community. They're just expediters, and their system is set up to move people and places in the same way that they'd move widgets, if that were their line. Their commission is paid by the seller, and naturally the seller just wants the best and quickest deal. Agents work from a hodgepodge list of buyers and sellers, and in order to survive in this very competitive and unpredictable business, they've got to write up as many purchase agreements as possible, ideally with minimal expenditure of effort. Like so many other professionals, they're just trying to make a living by maximizing their investment of time and talent. However, with a fresh look at this system, their time and talent could be better focused to solve real problems as a force for positive change, not merely as a finger on the invisible hand of the market.

WYNOTT OFFER SOME GUIDANCE?

Wynott depends on a healthy diversity to stay relevant, and Wynott real estate agents play a huge role in helping people to stay in their community, even as the size of their households expands and contracts.

Wynott nurtures and rewards agents who specialize in maintaining the vitality of the community. Motivated by a steady flow of Wy-Notes (and leads), these agents understand that a good fit means the right time and the right thing at the right place. Like seasoned matchmakers, they don't just find the best houses for people; they find the best people for houses. These agents are in tune with the market in this community, and they actively steer a healthy mix of families, singles, retirees, and you-name-them into the ideal properties. By recruiting a variety of households with the big picture in mind, Wynott agents help to manage the growth of neighborhoods. But most importantly, they work to keep people from leaving the neighborhood.

How do we accommodate this great mix of people in Wynott?

It's time to start infilling. The neighborhoods we've already got, from the core of the inner city to the shiniest new suburb, can be made more efficient.

WELCOME TO WYNOTT

Wynott isn't hostile to builders. Wynott beckons and encourages developers to rejuvenate our neighborhoods by turning existing lots into higher-density housing and mixed-use developments, infusing tired areas with new life and interesting density. Density means more connections, more people looking out for each other, more options.

By using *woonerfs* and getting creative with density, entire new developments can be built right inside the city. More shared common spaces and amenities, like play areas and community gardens, mean that homes can be smaller and more efficient, maximizing the square footage of both public and private spaces.

Every neighborhood should offer housing for its residents at all stages of their lives, economically and chronologically. With a blend of condos, townhomes, and apartments sprinkled in among the single-family homes, Wynott hosts all types of housing for all types of people. This means that whether you're a go-getting single, a new couple, a growing family, an empty nester, or a struggling young just-flown-the-nester, you can put down roots in one community and stay there comfortably for as long as you choose.

Low-income people have a place in Wynott. Diversity is the key to a strong society, and homogenization makes us vulnerable to disaster. When we corral all low-income people into a separate neighborhood of nothing but projects, we doom them to a life without hope. Few businesses will locate in that neighborhood. The children who grow up there see nothing but poverty. The only industry that has a fighting chance is crime. Despair takes over like a cancer. There's no reason for this. It's not the cost of building a house that makes it a low-income house; it's the lack of income from the buyers. The labor and the material cost the same, wherever you erect that house.

In Wynott, housing is available for a healthy mix of income levels and spread out to the point where the residents have lots of opportunities to find nearby employment, to access good education, and to form friendships and alliances with people in other income brackets. These opportunities are the keys to cutting short the cycle of poverty. Cutting out poverty benefits everyone in society by reducing the costs of health care, welfare, crime, and more.

Wynott is a great place to live, and none of its residents should be pushed out because their house has gotten too big or too small, or has too many stairs. The appeal of Wynott makes people willing to live with less square footage in exchange for higher quality of life: services, shops, and cafes within walking distance, a feeling of safety and familiarity, and a sense of community. The seniors who have the time and experience to do the most volunteering are the most attracted to a place like Wynott, where it is easy for them to get around and get their needs met. Seniors have an intense desire to remain independent, and it's a win-win situation to enable them to do so. By keeping and maintaining senior residents, Wynott can offer still more, offering them volunteer jobs with the kind of satisfaction and engagement that no activity center can rival.

When a place is filled with people who have a variety of strengths and needs, it means that there's a lot going on, a lot of potential there for the tapping. And when a place is filled with people who are excited to be there, who are loyal to their neighborhood and eager to stay there, it's a place that is succeeding.

> Seniors have an intense desire to remain independent, and it's a win-win situation to enable them to do so.

WHY CAN'T WE LIVE HIGHER THAN THE TREETOPS?

Imagine entering your kitchen with a bag of groceries, then pulling out your purchases and spreading them all over the counters and the floor. Imagine your whole kitchen is covered with boxes and cans and cartons, scattered in every direction. Now try making dinner. A kitchen arranged like that would be a very hard place in which to cook, which is why your kitchen has cupboards, maybe even a pantry. It's more efficient and logical to stack your groceries together in groups in designated central areas. But most of our American cities are neither as logical nor as efficient as your own kitchen. Housing is spread out all over, taking up way more space than necessary. It's as if each can of beans needs its own special hill.

When the sky is the limit, it makes more sense to build upward. Stack more stuff into less space. Keep a narrower footprint.

Manhattan, being an island, has to build upward. Cities constrained by coastlines or mountains that prevent them from spreading tend to be more willing (by necessity) to grow upward. But for some inexplicable reason, even as our population increases, many people have an aversion to buildings any higher than the treetops. Especially in the agrarian Midwest, where people are accustomed to being surrounded by 360 degrees of prairie. Cities like Minneapolis and Dallas, with no mountain or sea to hold them back, just keep sprawling out farther and farther.

Not only do people not want to live in buildings over three stories high, they don't want those buildings built in their neighborhoods. Negative associations haunt our imaginations, from the biblical Tower of Babel to high-rise low-income housing projects to the more recent attacks of September 11, 2001. Whether it's genuine fear or simple distaste, for a large segment of our population the theme song is "Don't Fence Me In." But of course, once we get our half-acre, the fence goes up pretty quickly.

As long as there are still cornfields for sale, builders will keep buying them and spreading homes all over them. Our wooded open spaces and our prime farmland are being consumed at an estimated rate of two million acres per year. In some areas, that's up to one acre per hour. By 2040, world population is projected to be nine billion, which means we can't afford to lay any more concrete over our cornfields—not if we want to eat.

WHERE WE LIVE

WYNOTT GROW UP?

High-density housing and mixed-use developments can revive failing city centers and bankrupt shopping malls while preserving agricultural space, forests, and wetlands.

But we can't just throw a high rise here, a high rise there, and call it a day. We don't want to merely redirect the builders into the city. We've got to reconsider not just where we build, but also *how* and *why*. We have an epidemic of *failure to plan*. We've been operating under the "if you build it they will come" impulse and not factoring in the lifecycles and maintenance of the structures we are building. Instead, the immediate return on investment is the only consideration. Sure, if you build it, they will come. And they will use what you build. And there will be wear and tear and problems and upkeep and maintenance expenses.

Old zoning laws that don't make sense any more must drop off the books or be rewritten to take into account the fact that the world has changed. Many changes have already been made, but the changes need to keep rolling.

City buildings have typically been planned according to or depending upon the number of available (or required) parking spaces. This is just crazy and completely unsustainable as well. Public transportation and other creative transportation solutions must fill the gap to support better density, more infill, and less sprawl.

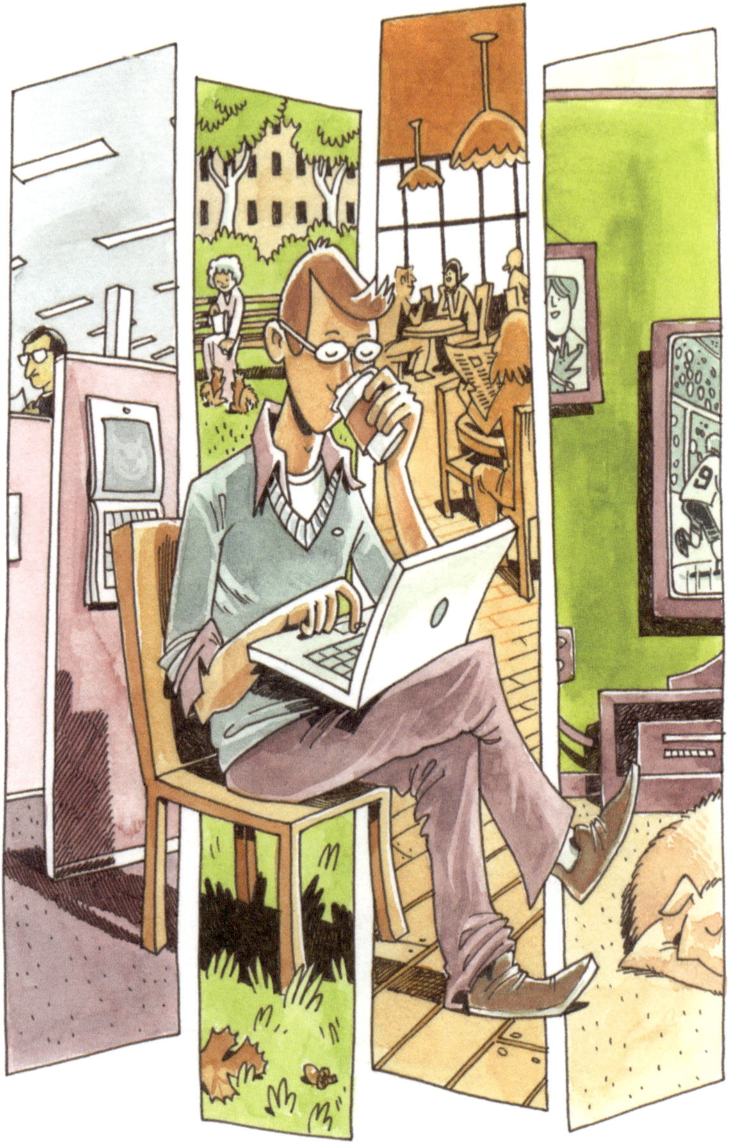

WHERE WE LIVE

Heavy industry is not what it used to be in America, and the zoning has to change to reflect that. In the information age, masses of American workers spend their workdays in meetings, on phones, and behind computers. And this work might not be accomplished "at work"—it might be done at home, on the road, in a coffee shop, in a hotel.

The virtual office makes it possible for us to work remotely and to stagger our work days and hours, thinning out rush-hour traffic. And our work itself has changed. Where industry once dominated, now most of us are employed in the information, technology, and service industries. On the whole, as a workforce we are now much more flexible. For many of us, our office can go anywhere we go or stay right where we stay.

Work is more mobile. Assembly lines are rarer. The physical reality of heavy industry no longer dictates our productive hours and seasons. We are returning, in a sense, to the era when there was less separation between work and home, between colleagues and families. On the family farm, your office extended as far as your fields stretched, and every able-bodied member of the family was part of the org chart. In town, the blacksmith, the baker, the grocer, the doctor, and even the sheriff might live and work in their own buildings, each with a shop or office up front and housing in back or up top. And just like on the farm, family members might be pressed into service.

WELCOME TO WYNOTT

The industrial age created major manufacturing centers, drawing workers from town and country. Work became a place to go to, separate from home life. Industrial areas were not the kind of places where people could live. Early factories were loud. They emitted terrible smells and great clouds of smoke and soot. Many were located on or near rivers, which were put to use running the mills. Riverside life was not considered as desirable then as it is now.

Consider the warehouse and industrial districts of many cities today. Generally located on rivers, these gloomy tracts of vast structures, abandoned by their first tenants, were next inhabited by squatters, artists, and bohemians who could afford little else. The artists made the most of the high ceilings and interesting industrial landscapes, transforming rejected buildings into hip and trendy locales. Gentrification began, and developers started scooping up cheap warehouses and transforming them into condos and restaurants. Riverfronts that once powered mills and carried away untreated waste and pollution are being restored and valued as parkland and natural resources. Brand-new developments designed to resemble old warehouse lofts are springing up in once-abandoned industrial districts all over America. The old polluted eyesores have now become some of the most valuable real estate in town, and the pesky vacant lots are being in-filled with the makings of the new urban village.

WHERE WE LIVE

These condos, lofts, and townhomes are drawing, of course, young urban professionals who want to live near to work, want to be part of the scene, close to the action. They're also drawing empty nesters, who are trading in the upkeep of a large suburban family home and yard for a more carefree (and maintenance-free) life in the city. And they're drawing new and growing families. They're drawing parents who don't want to waste hours each week commuting on congested highways; parents who want their kids to be immersed in a cultural scene; parents who are willing to exchange the quantity of square footage in a suburban tract home for the quality of life in an urban village.

We've reached the saturation point. The pendulum is swinging back.

There's a lifestyle shift occurring. People are choosing to bike, to walk, to take public transportation. Consumers are aware of where their dollars are going, what they are funding. They're conscientiously making spending decisions to support businesses that matter to them. People want to patronize their neighborhoods. And they want to live in neighborhoods that serve them, not merely their automobiles. People are social creatures, and as we spend less time together in the office, we find ways to spend more time together in public spaces. The social life is in the city. A city is designed to bring people together, whereas a suburb is designed to keep people apart.

WELCOME TO WYNOTT

We can't mandate where the builders build. We can't tell them to stop bulldozing cornfields and forests to build tract homes. And we don't have to tell them. The market will. It's already happening. A builder needs a substantial financial commitment by prospective buyers in order to start a new development, but the customers just aren't showing up anymore. There are already thousands of vacant new houses out in the suburbs that can't be sold. The large development companies are doing everything they can to entice people, but the demand has crested. That boom appears to be over.

The demand is shifting back to the city; but the builders there are facing problems similar to those of the builders in the suburbs. A builder needs a substantial financial commitment from prospective buyers before breaking ground or gutting a warehouse to turn it into condos. Even though demand is up, the average buyer can't make the necessary commitment until they sell the house they're currently in. The house they're currently in sits on the market for months and months. Where are these unsold houses? In the suburbs.

The shift is slow to occur. But it can't be denied—people are coming back to the city. Gas prices and drive times are a huge turn-off. And even though it's possible to work from home, which makes the long commute less of a downer, the new generation is still drawn to the city, *where there is no commute.*

WHERE WE LIVE

Quality of life ranks higher on the list. Young people want to be where the scene is, where the *character* is. They don't want to have to drive twenty minutes or more to get to the action. They are having children later, or not at all, and the conformity of the white picket fence doesn't serve the new generation of housing-seekers. The "Not-So-Big House" movement started by Sarah Susanka has tapped into the new breed of consumers who want to be inspired by their surroundings. They prioritize the quality of the square footage over the quantity.

This new breed of consumers seeks out locally grown foods and goods that aren't mass-produced in sweat shops. Unique shoe stores, boutique dress shops, and funky ethnic restaurants are finding their way back to the main drags and the downtowns. Specialized bakeries and butchers are seeing a revival. Neighborhood farmers' markets are blooming in vacant lots. They're run by entrepreneurs who don't have budgets for high-priced mall leases and who don't offer scale to meet supermarket demands. They're patronized by a new generation bored with the franchised conformity and the claustrophobic energy of the climate-controlled mall enclosures. People are asking "why?" And they're ready to hear "Wynott!"

A city neighborhood can incorporate the Wynott plan to become more of a village, and a suburb can incorporate the Wynott plan to become more urban.

WELCOME TO WYNOTT

A small town can use the Wynott plan to regenerate the magnetic strength of its once-mighty main street. Wynott takes that burgeoning rekindled desire for the city (the city as it was before white flight, the suburbs, and the highway system) and combines it with the better ideas of suburban living and the natural comforts and efficiencies of a small town. Wynott is the Urban Village.

WHY AREN'T WE TOOTING OUR HORNS?

When times are tough, a lot of companies cut back on marketing and promotional budgets. Then everybody forgets about these companies, forgets to patronize them, and they go away. Successful companies do the opposite—they actually increase their promotional budgets during stressful periods. They know that it's critical to keep their images and their messages alive when they're at their most vulnerable. A city is a lot like a company, and the budget is always getting squeezed. Promotional materials may seem pretty irrelevant, compared to, say, police or sewers, so they are often the first budget line to get cut. But perception is reality, and as the saying goes, attitude determines the altitude.

Without a steady flow of good news, human-interest stories, coverage of events and happenings, and some good old-fashioned boosterism, what's left is the bad news. Bad news happens every day, everywhere, and it makes headlines. If bad news is the only news you hear about a neighborhood, it can define a place. Before long, it seems like the only time you hear about your neighborhood is when there's a crime attached to it. That doesn't feel good.

When people don't feel good about their city, or their neighborhood, they have less pride. They spend less time taking care of their property. They leave the litter, they don't pick up after dogs, they don't make repairs or plant flowers. One or two unkempt homes on a block bring down the value of the others and invite graffiti and vandals. People feel less secure walking the streets and sidewalks. They lose interest in nearby businesses and restaurants. Lack of citizen engagement makes it easier for drug dealers, gangs, and other criminals to get a foothold and operate comfortably.

The people who can afford to get out, get out. They disinvest in the place by moving to "better" neighborhoods, pulling their kids out of the schools, their money out of the local businesses, their energy out of the community. They move to a place that makes them feel good and safe. Attractive businesses disinvest by moving out to where the action is better. They leave behind empty storefronts or are replaced by businesses that prey on struggling populations: payday lenders, stores that sell nothing but cigarettes and junk food, high-interest rent-to-own furniture dealers.

WELCOME TO WYNOTT

Bad news brings more bad news. The media picks up on problems and magnifies them, milking out every salacious detail to boost their own ratings. The story of one carjacking is played out and repeated until it seems like every guy you pass on the street is plotting to steal your car. Every house is a meth lab. Every teen is a gangbanger. The fear feeds on itself and creates a climate of hostility and distrust.

> **The minute folks get a whiff of a neighborhood going downhill, it does go downhill, rapidly.**

And everybody loses. The minute folks get a whiff of a neighborhood going downhill, it does go downhill, rapidly. There's no demand, so people walk away from it. Disinvest. Nobody wants to visit, which means businesses generate less revenue. More crime takes up more police time and more of the budget. Sinking property values means a lower tax base, which means the city has to go back to their budget and make some more cuts. At this point, promotion is the last thing on anyone's mind. What's left to promote?

WYNOTT SPREAD THE GOOD WORD?

Have you ever looked at pictures of houses for sale and been struck by how an ordinary-looking house in one neighborhood seems to cost a fortune, but a nearly identical house in a different part of town might go for just a fraction of that price? The price is dictated by the three rules of real estate: location, location, location. And location can be radically different within just a few miles. The two houses have the same climate, they're in the same metropolitan area, but one is in a neighborhood that is considered desirable, and the other is not.

"Desirable" itself changes. It's not unusual for a town or a neighborhood to rise, fall, and rise again. Booms and busts, shifting demographics, changes in architectural taste, crime waves, and gentrification can affect an area. A grand neighborhood can get down on its luck, and all of its tony homes will slowly deteriorate. Many of them will be transformed into cramped, cheap apartments, until a few starving artists come in and start restoring them to their former glory, and suddenly it's valuable again. Put up a factory, close down a factory, transform a factory into condos. Add a park, add a landfill. Run a highway through it. Cut down all of the trees. Move in some great ethnic restaurants. Relocate an airport. The variables are endless, but no matter what happens externally, the perception of a place is the most important factor.

WELCOME TO WYNOTT

Perception can be managed.

The same house, the same yard, the same street can feel like a completely different place with just a small shift in perspective. When people hear nothing but bad news about where they live, they stay inside, huddled around their TVs and computers with the doors locked. And so it becomes less safe, less valuable. As it becomes less desirable, it generates and attracts undesirable businesses and activities. But, when folks hear the good news about where they live, they get out and mingle, work in the yard, chat with the neighbors, stay in tune with the comings and goings of their block and the blocks beyond. And so it becomes safer and more valuable. And as it becomes more desirable, it generates and attracts more desirable businesses and activities. When everybody wants to be there, it means vitality, diversity, and opportunity.

Image and reputation are self-fulfilling prophecies. If you think your neighborhood is bad, it is; you want to get out and so does everyone else. If you think your neighborhood is good, it is; you want to stay, and other people are attracted to it. Managing the image and reputation of a community is vital to its success. And the good news is, it's not that hard to talk about good news.

The good news is, it's not that hard to talk about good news.

Wynott has an advertising budget and a marketing plan that plays up the highlights of the area. When you brag up the place and get a little momentum going, suddenly everybody wants to be there. It's like that old joke about the graveyard—"Why do they need a fence? Because everybody's dying to get in!"

It doesn't take very much to get momentum started. A few press releases and a website will get the ball rolling. A social networking site can start connecting people who live on the same street but have yet to meet face to face, and the very same technology that keeps people locked in the house can be used to get neighbors informed and involved and bring people together. As awareness grows, Wynott takes on a life of its own, and a personality emerges.

The character and personality of Wynott brings out the personality of the residents who identify with their chosen location. They paint their houses, they put flowers out in the window boxes, and they keep things looking spiffy and inviting. They're proud to be part of the scene, and they're invested in what happens next. Which means that they get involved, they pitch in, and they're active. The success of Wynott becomes a self-fulfilling prophecy—the better it seems, the better it gets.

The people who are drawn to live in Wynott are the people with hope and optimism, and soon that hope and optimism spreads. It feels like a privilege to be here. It feels lucky. It just feels good.

8

What We Learn

WHY DO WE LET CHILDREN BECOME GANGSTERS?

Police can find the bad guys, catch the bad guys, and foil the bad guys' plans, but the bad guys still exist, and there will never be a police force large enough to stop crime altogether. The police do, however, have a pretty good idea of what can prevent crime: the Alphabet Song. Turns out that high-quality early childhood care and education is the most powerful weapon we have against the criminal population.

WHAT WE LEARN

The nonprofit anti-crime organization *Fight Crime: Invest in Kids* is made up of more than five thousand police chiefs, sheriffs, prosecutors, attorneys general, and other law-enforcement leaders, as well as survivors of violence. Their own expertise, coupled with the overwhelming evidence of plain statistics, leads them to fight for changes that really make a difference. In their own words, "We are committed to putting dangerous criminals behind bars. But by the time law enforcement get involved, the damage is already done and lives are changed forever." This is why they're dedicated to early childhood education and other efforts aimed at giving kids the help they need to make the right choices in life.

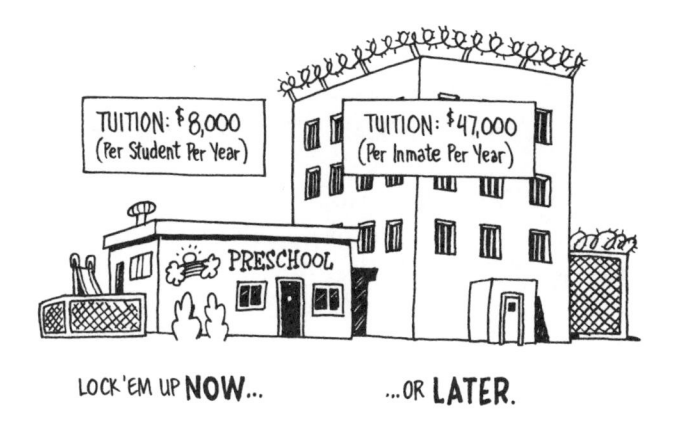

LOCK 'EM UP **NOW**... ...OR **LATER**.

The nature vs. nurture verdict is still out, but it has been proven that a large percentage of criminals are not born, but rather made—by neglect, abuse, bad training, and lack of better options. In areas of high poverty and limited opportunity, children who do not attend preschool are up to 70 percent more likely to be arrested for a violent crime by age eighteen. That's right—VIOLENT crime. We're not talking stealing hubcaps.

There is value to putting more police on the streets. A more robust force means that the ne'er-do-well is more quickly apprehended or else looks for criminal opportunity elsewhere. Every dollar spent on a cop saves four dollars in crime costs on that cop's beat. However, when it comes to early childhood education, the savings turns out to be *sixteen dollars* for every dollar spent. The return on investment is quadrupled, and it's not limited, geographically, to one cop's beat.

WYNOTT LISTEN TO THE EXPERTS?

It's just a lot easier and a lot cheaper—and feels much better—to keep people from becoming criminals than it is to keep criminals from committing crime. In the words of Los Angeles County Sheriff Leroy Baca, "We need to step up and invest in what works to keep America's most vulnerable children from becoming America's most-wanted adults."

For the best return on investment in crime-fighting dollars, Wynott spends money on prevention. We

WHAT WE LEARN

get more kids finger painting at age three, so we can spend less time fingerprinting them at age thirteen, twenty-three, and thirty. What is this earth-shattering, revolutionary solution? Early education.

Wynott starts with early childhood education to build a solid foundation, and continues on through childhood and teen years by giving kids more school hours to build success. Stimulating activities and social opportunities are provided for teens who might otherwise be adrift. It's the kids with too much time on their hands and with nothing more interesting to do who end up as delinquents and hoodlums. In Wynott, children always have something interesting to do, which gives them less time for and interest in petty crime.

The upshot is, we need to get kids educated early and often.

WELCOME TO WYNOTT

WHY DO AMERICAN STUDENTS SPEND LESS TIME IN SCHOOL THAN ANYONE ELSE?

Discussion gets heated when talk turns to longer school terms, as if the hallowed three-month summer vacation had been handed down to Moses with the Ten Commandments. But very little of our modern education system has been around for more than a century. Consider the age-grade system—you know, kindergarten, first grade, and so on. That didn't exist before 1848. Children used to just show up at school and attend as many terms as they were able, without being grouped into ages. The radical Quincy Grammar School in Boston, Massachusetts introduced the age-grade system to America, and it rapidly caught on.

Up until then, rural schools had featured fall and spring breaks for farm work. Industrialized city schools let children out during the hot, unproductive summer months to coincide with the factory downtimes. Eventually, as age-grading became the norm, a nationwide summer break was instituted as a way of ensuring that everyone was on the same schedule, that all of the fourth graders were starting and ending fourth grade at the same time. It worked well enough, because most children had a mother at home to mind them over the long summer.

It made sense, at one time, to organize our school year around the needs of farms and factories, but that's no longer a reality. Unless their parents are teachers, most students come from families where one or

WHAT WE LEARN

both parents work eight hours a day, 250 days a year. Compare that to six-hour school days, 180 days a year, which includes a three-month summer break. And in the southern edge of our nation, being sent out to play during the stifling hot summer months might seem more like a punishment than a privilege. Nationwide, the three-month break leaves most families with a big fat daycare bill. Or it means latchkey kids are left unsupervised with little to do but watch TV for several hours each week, all summer long. With students having shorter days than their working parents, there's often an unsupervised after-school gap of a few hours. Best-case scenario, kids watch a lot of *Sponge Bob*. Worst-case scenario, the boredom leads to mischief and delinquency.

WELCOME TO WYNOTT

The way we work has dramatically changed since 1848, but our school structure is stuck in a time warp. Families are smaller and living farther apart, usually with no older siblings or grandmothers at home to help with childcare. Having one full-time stay-at-home parent has now become a luxury in our society. At the same time, our workplace has become more flexible. More workers can telecommute, working part or most of the time from home, making different school schedules more of a possibility.

And yet, despite computers, commuters, smartphones, and flex time, we stubbornly cling to a schedule that was cutting edge, oh, 150 years ago. Now, for three long months every summer, kids are removed from academic structure and forget a good chunk of their learning. If their family has the resources, they'll go from camp to camp, possibly packing in some more knowledge. If their family doesn't, they'll just hang out and experience the summer brain drain that further separates the haves from the have-nots and makes teachers' jobs so much harder every autumn.

When school starts up again in the fall, staff and students must acclimate to each other, and to the new schedule. Time is spent refreshing facts and concepts that have been forgotten. Conversely, as vacation approaches every spring, the students get squirrely, which makes for a few weeks of unproductive classroom

WHAT WE LEARN

time. Add those unproductive spring and fall weeks to a whole summer of downtime, and we're just not getting our money's worth.

If Americans were dominating the world's education scene, we could afford to let our kids' brains go dormant for the 920 extra hours per year that the Asian nations dedicate to learning. But we're not doing so hot. We don't need our kids at home to plow the back forty, and the assembly line work has all been outsourced, so if we want them to be able to buy groceries someday, we need to invest more time in their education. No corporation in the world would run such an inefficient operation.

WELCOME TO WYNOTT

WYNOTT SPEND MORE ON EDUCATION AND LESS ON CABLE AND DAYCARE?

Wynott has school year round, with longer days and more frequent weeklong breaks to recharge. Year-round school means that kids have more time to learn and teachers have more time to teach. Because when it comes to education, quantity IS quality. This kind of schedule offers more consistency for students and creates a pattern more like that of their parents' work and their own future careers.

> ... when it comes to education, quantity IS quality.

While we're reorganizing our school year, let's do it right. Let's do away with the arbitrary September 1 cutoff date most schools use to determine who starts kindergarten. This cutoff date means that a child born on August 31 can start kindergarten as a very young five-year-old, but a kid born the very next day, on September 1, will be held back and start school one year later as a tall six-year-old. These two kids, born a day apart, should be in school together.

Let's put a true quarterly system into place and start each incoming kindergarten class with kids born during the same time span. All of the kids with fall birthdays start kindergarten in the fall, the winter birthdays start in winter, spring in spring, and summer in summer. Any educator—and any parent—will tell you that a few months can make a big difference

WHAT WE LEARN

in maturity, especially in the early grades. If a child is particularly advanced or not quite ready, she or he can be allowed to start in a different quarter. As children progress through the grades, they can move up or back by quarters to be with the optimal learning group. Going back a quarter is not a big deal—but being held back a whole year is a shame, a stigma, and a waste of everyone's time. Flexibility should be the key, and a year is an eternity in the development of a child. When there's always a new quarter starting, it gives students a chance to jump forward or to painlessly repeat the most recent learning and really solidify it.

If a student—or a teacher!—desperately needs and wants a three-month break, they can take a quarter off. Summer vacation is still within the realm of possibility, but would probably be used less frequently, like a sabbatical.

In this country, once again, Boston, Massachusetts is pioneering a radical new school system, with a calendar that better meets the needs of today's students and their families. By extending both the length and the number of school days, the Expanded Learning Time Initiative has added three hundred hours to the school year of its pilot schools, and the results are stunning. A low-achieving Boston middle school went from the brink of closing to becoming an academic star school with a waiting list of students eager to get in. In the space of three years, their test scores zoomed up and teacher satisfaction surpassed that of their peers across the state. Because students in such schools get more personalized instruction and longer blocks of learning time, they are able to improve in core studies and also choose electives that excite them. Because of the pilot school's success, every Boston public middle school has now applied to participate in the Expanded Learning Time Initiative.

Other schools around the country are working on a four-season quarterly schedule. They have the same number of school days as standard schools, but it's split up so that at the end of each quarter, students and staff get a good long break. They also offer "inter-sessions" that give kids additional educational opportunities during breaks, much like summer school or enrichment learning. Parents with kids on this schedule love the fact that they don't have to hustle to fill up a whole summer with activities. They also have more flexibility to plan a quality family vacation that doesn't always fall in the crowded tourist season. Students are refreshed by the frequent breaks—long enough to relax and recharge, but not so long that they forget everything they've just learned.

WHY DO WE EXPECT OUR TEACHERS TO DO WHAT WE CAN'T DO?

Thirty-five kids. Eight with runny noses. Seven who can't tie their shoes. Six who didn't eat breakfast

WHAT WE LEARN

this morning. Five who left their homework at daycare. Four who forgot to take their ADHD meds. Three who just moved here from a different district with different standards. Two whose parents are in the middle of a divorce. And one teacher.

Do the math.

Teachers need help. Smaller class size is critical to success, but shrinking budgets and consolidating school districts mean that the teachers who get to keep their jobs are expected to do more with less—less of everything but students.

WELCOME TO WYNOTT

In Wynott we want our kids to get a better education; a deeper, richer, longer education. But we can't do it with the same number of teachers getting paid the same salary. If we are gonna give them more to do, we've gotta give them more to do it with.

WYNOTT GIVE TEACHERS CREDIT?

Credit. Cash. Wy-Notes. However we can pay them what they're worth, in Wynott we will do it. By seeking out public-private partnerships, grants, and every possible source of funding, we invest in our education system, and we are not afraid to fairly compensate the dedicated professionals who educate.

Rewarding excellence is our motto. Attracting excellence is our secret weapon.

We make things good for teachers, so that good teachers will be competing for a chance to work here. It starts with simple respect. In Wynott, teachers have status. Teaching is a higher calling. A rare few of us hear that call. Those who do must be supported.

Wynott supports teachers by putting an army of volunteers at their disposal. Retirees and others are aggressively recruited and trained to serve and aid classrooms and to lighten the teachers' loads. Everyone in the community—not just the ones with kids in school—is called upon to pitch in and make our

WHAT WE LEARN

education system more efficient. Helping out in the classrooms, sweeping floors at night, making copies, leading activities—these jobs and more can be done by volunteers to help stretch the budget and to give educators more time and space to do their best.

WHY DO WE FEED OUR KIDS CRAP FOOD IN SCHOOL LUNCHROOMS?

If we give students substandard fuel at lunchtime, we may as well be giving them broken pencils and math books with missing pages. They can't learn without the proper tools, and that includes good nutrition. National standards, farm subsidies, and tight school budgets mean that dollar for dollar, the average school lunch is worth less than a cup of coffee. Processed foods loaded with salt, sugar, and fat contribute to childhood obesity and inhibit children's ability to focus and learn. In her 1996 essay, *Slow Food, Slow Schools: Transforming Education Through a School Lunch Curriculum*, food reformer Alice Waters gets to the core of the problem. "In school cafeterias, students learn how little we care about the way they nourish themselves—we've sold them to the lowest bidder. Soda machines line the hallways. At best we serve them government-subsidized agricultural surplus, at worst we invite fast food restaurants to open on school grounds."

The students eating these meals are on target to become the first generation in America to have a shorter life expectancy than their parents.

For many students, the subsidized school lunch is the best meal they'll get all day. But even though they're undernourished, they're overweight. Obesity, once an indicator of wealth and good living, is now the epidemic of the poor, whose diet of low-cost processed food increases their vulnerability to heart disease and diabetes. If current trends continue, the Center for Disease Control expects one in three children to develop diabetes sometime in their lifetime, losing, on average, ten to fifteen years of life per person, and costing our population $174 billion in total.

There are people all over this issue right now pushing for change, including First Lady Michelle Obama. Celebrity Chef Jamie Oliver gave British school lunches a makeover and has now turned his attention to American cafeterias. The Edible Schoolyard, created by Alice Waters, turned blacktop into a garden where students work, learn, and grow food for their own lunches.

Every moment that a child is in school is part of an education, and lunch is no exception.

Every moment that a child is in school is part of an education, and lunch is no exception. When they finish school, they may not be called upon again to use algebra or the details of the Spanish–American War, but they'll be putting food into their mouths several times a day, every day, for the rest of their waking lives.

WYNOTT MAKE LUNCH PART OF THE SOLUTION INSTEAD OF PART OF THE PROBLEM?

In Wynott, learning doesn't stop at lunchtime. Students are involved in budget decisions. They learn where their food comes from, and how it is distributed and prepared. They discover which foods offer the best nutritional value for their growing bodies, and they take turns preparing food in the kitchen. By incorporating these lessons into their school day, they'll be educated on a topic that will always be relevant to them.

When students are active participants in planning menus, they become their own advocates for better food choices.

The lunch hour in Wynott is at least forty minutes long, not a mere twenty minutes, and lunch doesn't start, like in some insanely overcrowded schools, at 9:30 a.m. Kids don't bolt down a meal and then run out to play. First they go to recess and work up an appetite, then they come in and eat. School lunch in Wynott nourishes both the body and the mind.

WELCOME TO WYNOTT

WHY DO WE ERECT AND MAINTAIN EXPENSIVE SCHOOL BUILDINGS THAT ARE USED LESS THAN 20% OF THE TIME?

In America, students and staff occupy the average school building for 1,620 hours a year. That means that for 7,140 hours a year, some of our best public facilities sit empty. No one is using the classrooms, the offices, the gym, the cafeteria, or the auditorium. The tracks, fields, playgrounds, and pools are quiet. The parking lot is a vast stretch of empty asphalt. The insurance coverage is paid for, the heat is on, the lights are on, but nobody's there.

> ... for 7,140 hours a year, some of our best public facilities sit empty.

Yes, many schools host after-hours scout meetings, community ed classes, elections, and some nonschool sports events and entertainment. But there's still a lot of room to spare, with the benefit of sharing maintenance and utility costs.

Yeah, yeah, yeah, it all sounds pretty nifty, but what about the liability? The conflicts of interest? The miles and miles of red tape? It just isn't done, is it? It is, actually. And not in some distant country or far-out cult compound, but right here, in American cities, suburbs, and rural areas. We're turning the tables on school buildings.

WHAT WE LEARN

WYNOTT MAKE THE SCHOOLHOUSE ROCK?

Some of the most innovative educational facilities currently share spaces with organizations whose missions enhance or improve learning. Museums are partnering with schools in New York, Washington, DC, Michigan, Arizona, and Minnesota, to name a few. Every day feels like a field trip as students are enriched by inspirational surroundings, deep resources of knowledge, and apprenticeship opportunities. Zoos and environmental centers have made room for fulltime students in Hawaii, North Carolina, Nebraska, and elsewhere, resulting in classrooms where kids are always curious and always involved. Across the country, libraries and schools are becoming more efficient by sharing space with each other, giving students greater access to materials, and enabling beleaguered libraries to stay open for longer hours. It's win-win all around as schools get enriched environments, cultural institutions get a hand in developing the next generation of patrons, and everybody saves a few dollars.

Daycares, social services, health clinics, senior care facilities, and government agencies are all buddying up with K–12 schools across the United States. Radical as all of this streamlined efficiency seems, it's no more revolutionary than the one-room frontier schoolhouse, which also served as town hall, church, makeshift clinic, and dance floor.

WELCOME TO WYNOTT

It doesn't stop there. At the Metropolitan Learning Alliance located in the Mall of America, high-school students mix liberal arts studies with business lessons that are played out in real time in the surrounding retail environment. This one may be the biggest, but it's not the only mall that's home to a school. All over the United States, retail and business centers are making space for students.

It's a no-brainer for any new or expanding school to consider partnering with other organizations to share space. But solutions come in many shapes and sizes. A school that's burdened by budget-breaking maintenance and repair costs can learn a lesson from Perham, Minnesota. The problem of a run-down high-school gymnasium led to the building of a new community fitness center attached to the school. This vibrant gathering spot is open seven days a week, from early in the morning to late at night, and is enjoyed by all ages, improving both the quality and cost of living in a small town with a small budget.

All of these creative solutions maximize space, minimize costs, and supersize learning opportunities. But you don't have to build a new facility, add on a new wing, or relocate your students to get more out of your school. Any school building can give you

> Any school building can give you more bang for the buck … just look what you've got to work with.

WHAT WE LEARN

more bang for the buck by becoming a cultural, entrepreneurial, community hub. Just take a look at what you've got to work with.

How about that nice big stainless steel kitchen, for instance? For 190 days a year, it serves two meals a day. It's routinely inspected by the Department of Health and features commercial-grade equipment. Now imagine that you've got a prizewinning family pickle recipe, and you'd like to make some batches to sell in your local grocery store. The store is willing to stock it, but the pickles must be prepared in a licensed kitchen, which you don't own and couldn't possibly afford. What you might do instead is go to an incubator kitchen.

The incubator kitchen movement is enabling small vendors and artisans to prepare their wares in licensed commercial kitchens. Mostly restaurants, these kitchens rent out unused blocks of time to keep overhead low and to give small producers a way into the market. In St. Paul, Minnesota, for instance, a small bakery did the math and figured that their facility went unused two thirds of the time. They started renting out timeslots, and now small-scale almond roasters, hummus makers, and nutrition-bar bakers keep the kitchens operating at full capacity and help pay the rent.

Why not in our schools? Once lunch is served, the vast kitchen is empty, and the long lunch tables (which make handy packaging surfaces) are bare. With ample

WELCOME TO WYNOTT

downtime and capacity, school kitchens could be turning out sauces, compotes, couscous, tamales, caramels, cinnamon rolls, baby food, soups, and gluten-free trail mix. They could house caterers getting ready for weekend weddings. They could pickle peppers throughout vacation breaks. They could also serve as prep sites for food banks and charities. Chefs without restaurants could teach classes, test recipes, and develop menus. And in the right set of circumstances, the students eating lunch at that school could learn about local foods. They could have the opportunity to study entrepreneurs' business plans and possibly assist with the work. A budgetary assist leads to one teachable moment after another.

How many other small start-ups or nonprofits could office out of existing educational spaces? Why do most school buildings sit vacant 80 percent of the time, and what can we do about it?

A Wynott school building is never underutilized. Here are ten ideas for starters:

1. Turn our school's valuable and underused licensed commercial kitchen into a moneymaker that supports local businesses and models entrepreneurship to students.

2. Transform our school's gymnasium, field, cafeteria, or parking lot into a regular weekend

WHAT WE LEARN

farmers' market/swap meet/art fair/flea market/craft show/bazaar.

3. Partner with local theater companies, dance troupes, musicians, and other performing artists to offer reasonably priced after-hours rehearsal and performance space, or free space in exchange for student arts education opportunities.

4. Inventory specialized equipment and facilities (wood shop, mechanics shop, screening or recording equipment, swimming pools) and rent them out.

5. Host after-hours immunization clinics, eye exams, acupuncture treatment, chiropractic care, massage therapy, or any kind of portable health services.

6. Offer open green space or roof space to local gardeners.

7. Open up the gym on nights and weekends for yoga classes, belly dancers, kickboxers, and hip-hoppers.

ESL
WEEKEND HOSTEL
SWAP MEET
Aa Bb Cc Dd
YOGA
OM...
OM...
OM...
OM...
SPECIALTY KITCHEN
WOODWORKING CLASS
WYNOTT ELEMENTARY SCHOOL

WHAT WE LEARN

8. Allow promoters to hold summer concerts and parties on campus.

9. Rent parking spaces to RV travelers for limited hours on school days, longer stretches on weekends and breaks. Charge a premium for bathroom access.

10. Invest in a few cots and become a youth or elder hostel on vacation days. Sell travelers food from the kitchen.

How many great ideas remain to be explored? Convergence can happen in any school building. These underused structures are the natural centers of the community and should be used to their full potential!

In Wynott, from the lunchroom to the classroom, the school is operated in a way that makes more sense to modern needs, that's up to date with modern research, and that prepares today's children for a modern world. It maximizes both time and money. And because it's a great school with great results, it does what all great schools do—it draws people into the community, builds a demand, and increases property values.

WELCOME TO WYNOTT

WHY DO WE THINK WE'RE DONE LEARNING?

So you've got a degree or some kind of trade, and somebody's giving you a paycheck for it. Yeah? Well, so what?

In a changing job climate, it's vital for workers to always be learning new skills. The technology moves so fast, and the needs change so quickly, that if you don't keep up you'll be left behind. We can't begin to predict what we'll be called upon to do tomorrow.

Professions that once seemed rock solid can vanish into history. One hundred years ago, a prudent young man might consider blacksmithing as a sensible career choice: a steady, well-paid job for 3,500 years running. Now, a blacksmith is lucky to find work as an exhibit at the Renaissance festival.

We wouldn't counsel any young person today to become a blacksmith, but we'd surely recommend doctor, lawyer, or accountant. However, as Daniel Pink points out in his book *A Whole New Mind,* doctors are losing patients to the computer. Years and years of med school and experience are being replaced by WebMD and other online services, which quickly track symptoms and diagnose problems. Patients who would once schlep themselves into a clinic, only to be told to drink fluids and rest, are now checking online first and saving themselves a trip and a bill. Lawyers are losing work to efficient online contract templates that can be easily downloaded for a small fee. All of those

WHAT WE LEARN

simple contracts, which used to be their bread and butter, have gone away, and lawyers have to hustle a little harder to make up for it. The CPAs who once prepared taxes around the clock from January to April are being replaced by the incredibly popular TurboTax software. While a boon for taxpayers, it's been a huge drain on the CPA industry.

What this means is that the majority of the quick-money clients are taking care of themselves, and lawyers, doctors, and accountants are now left with only the most complicated and time-consuming cases. And not only is the work getting harder, there's also less of it to go around. The low-hanging fruit is gone. New technology has siphoned off the easiest parts of so many left-brained jobs.

No one's career is secure. Enron. Arthur Anderson. Lehman Brothers. Borders. Those names used to inspire confidence. Now we can only shake our heads. For one astonishing reason or another, these once-unsinkable employers disappeared nearly overnight, like so many *Titanic*s steering into icebergs. The thousands of confident workers these employers comfortably employed were left to sink or swim, with a severe shortage of lifeboats.

That wouldn't happen to *your* company, you think. Your company has it going on. Maybe so, but your individual career isn't even secure at a perfectly healthy organization. Corporations are constantly cutting and shifting, trimming fat, ever focused on the bottom line. One day you're running the meeting, the next day you're clearing out your cube and being escorted to your car by a security guard.

Budget cuts, takeovers, and changing demographics put teachers, cops, pilots, and librarians out of work. Advances in health care and longer life expectancy for today's senior citizens means that even the undertakers are hustling to meet quotas.

Rare is the worker, these days, with true job security. Only the nimble survive.

Only the nimble survive. People need to stay flexible, and be ready to adapt, migrate, or innovate as required by the circumstance. People need to keep their minds open and their brains clicking. People need to continue learning.

WYNOTT GO BACK TO SCHOOL?

In Wynott the learning never stops. People in the community are called upon to share their expertise with others. With Wy-Notes as tuition, formal and informal classes are always being offered and attended. Lifelong learning is the way of life in this community.

Retirees are sought to teach classes and impart the knowledge they've gained during the length and

WHAT WE LEARN

breadth of their careers. Retirees are also taught the latest skills by the up-and-coming tech-savvy generation. Getting and keeping a paycheck is just one reason to keep learning. Getting and keeping a brain, an imagination, a life, a social network, is just as valid, if not more so.

More than anything, the culture of Wynott builds the positive peer pressure to never stop learning and never stop teaching. The classroom is everywhere, and it's always in session.

9

What We Buy

WHY BUY ONE AT A TIME?

Imagine you're alone in a restaurant, and you've been waiting and waiting and waiting for a simple plate of spaghetti. At last it arrives, and you dig in with gusto. It tastes just fine. Before long you've cleaned your plate, and it's time to pay the check. You glance at the total, and can't believe your eyes: $97.00!

You summon the waiter.

YOU: I think there's some mistake with my bill.

WAITER: Oh no, that's the correct price.

YOU: For spaghetti?

WAITER: There were ninety-seven noodles on your plate, and at one dollar per noodle—

YOU: It's pasta! Pasta costs pennies to make!

WAITER: Maybe so, but we buy *our* pasta individually wrapped. It takes our staff hours just to unpackage one serving. And then, of course, we must prepare ninety-seven separate pots of boiling water—

A restaurant like this could never stay in business. We would never agree to pay for individually packaged, individually prepared spaghetti noodles. And yet, every day we pay for customized, individualized products and services that would cost much less and entail less hassle if we could leverage the economy of scale.

WYNOTT PACKAGE YOUR PASTA?

You get more bang for your buck in Wynott, because Wynott is not an island. Wynott reaches out to neighboring communities, and in every way possible streamlines services and shares inventories. Instead of buying one noodle at a time, Wynott says, "Hey, everybody, let's all go in on a big box of pasta and have a nice dinner!"

Economy of scale is the way to go. Wynott doesn't spend money on expensive equipment that's only used a few times in one season. It shares the costs and benefits

WELCOME TO WYNOTT

with the next town over. Wynott combines with surrounding communities to get good deals on grass seed, paper towels, lightbulbs, lumber, and Internet service. Wynott shares administrative and maintenance workers and facilities, plus audit and inventory control services, and aggressively seeks out ways to be efficient and cost-effective.

Maybe Wynott has a really great bike trail, and the next town over has a bird sanctuary. The two can join forces and share the costs and responsibilities of maintaining, promoting, and administering these local amenities, which certainly draw visitors from both towns as well as from farther out.

This attitude permeates throughout. Neighborhoods join forces and form networks to enjoy the efficiency of combined services. If you live in Wynott, you are encouraged to offer a discount or some other form of incentive to others in the community. Whether you are an architect, a lawyer, an electrician, or a manicurist, you stand to benefit by building a clientele close to home. The savings of your marketing and transportation costs can be passed on to your Wynott clients, who will give you word-of-mouth recommendations.

A local plumbing company, for instance, contracts to service one area exclusively. Individuals are free to participate or not; no one will be stopped from using their old plumber. But for those who want in, this particular local plumber is always on call in the

WHAT WE BUY

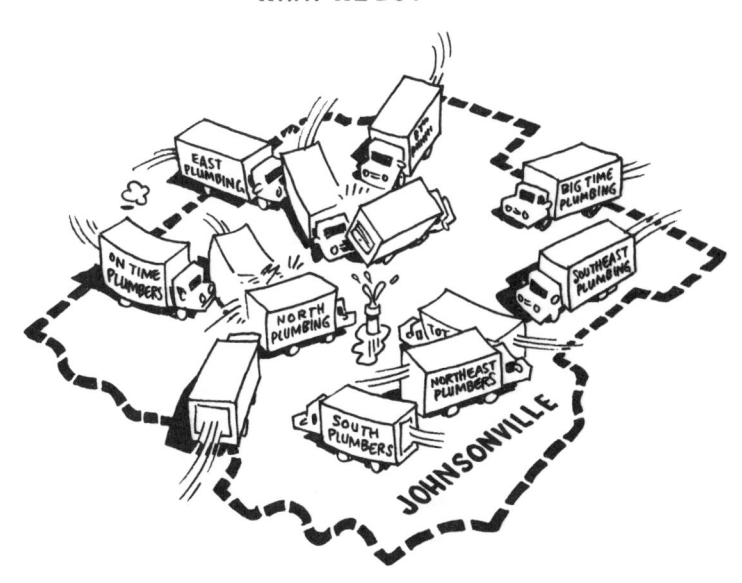

neighborhood and charges a lower rate for those locals who choose to join the network. Guaranteed business, reduced travel time and costs, and reduced advertising expenses create savings that the plumber can pass on to the network. And even though customers pay a bit less, they actually get better service and reliability. Because this company is always in the neighborhood, they can arrive quickly. They get to know people by name and familiarize themselves the quirks of these particular houses, buildings, pipes, and systems. Now they're the area specialists, able to offer higher-quality service. They buy parts in bulk and split the costs across the network. And this plumbing company will endeavor to keep customers highly satisfied, because if they provide poor service more than a few times, they won't just lose one customer, they'll lose a whole network.

Not only does this save money for people in the neighborhood, but it binds them together. With this connection established, it's a no-brainer to seek out other ways to buy in bulk and save. Now not just cities but neighbors are joining forces to get good deals on grass seed, paper towels, lightbulbs, lumber, and Internet service. With trust established and the financial savings realized, it gets easier to share lawn mowers, table saws, steam cleaners, and any number of items that take up space and aren't used on a daily basis. This frees up both storage space and money, enhancing the quality of life for Wynott residents. Some of them may even opt to share an automobile . . .

WHY DO WE PUT UP WITH LOUSY SERVICE?

There's an old joke about two public works employees who were busy with their shovels on a city boulevard. The first worker would dig a deep hole, and then the second worker would follow behind and fill it right back up again. All day long they toiled in this way, up one street and down the next. Finally, a curious passerby stopped to make conversation. "You guys are obviously working very hard, but I just don't get it—why do you dig holes, only to fill them back up again?"

The first digger cheerfully explained, "Well, normally we're a three-man team, but the guy who plants the trees is sick today."

The problem with many public jobs is that the system rewards excellence and incompetence equally. If you punch your timecard often enough and fulfill the bare minimum of duties required of you, it's possible to be promoted and given tenure, regardless of your accomplishments or lack thereof. There's not much benefit to thinking creatively and finding more efficient ways to get things done. MOST PEOPLE will do their best regardless, because that's the kind of stuff they're made of. But it doesn't always mean they'll be allowed to rise much higher or get paid much better than the layabout colleague who does the same job.

The private sector isn't always better, either. The same thing happens in a union that refuses to evolve and insists on protecting the underachievers within its ranks. Or when a property management company spreads their employees too thin and offers no incentive or recognition for competence and dedication.

Why go out of your way to solve a problem? All it means is more work for you, and you aren't obligated to do anything beyond the orders given. "I'm just paid to fill the holes—I don't plant the trees. That's some other guy's job."

It's not just about more work, either; changing the status quo could actually lead to less work. In so many ways, these workers are actually given a *disincentive* to provide quality service. If you are too efficient, if things run too smoothly, if you make it all look too easy, that means we can cut some jobs and squeeze more work out of a smaller staff.

There's plenty of disincentive, but so often there's also a disconnect. A person doesn't have to live in a building to manage it. You don't have to live in a city to work there. It's perfectly okay to get in and get out; leave work behind and forget all about it at the end of the day. But when a guy is digging holes on his own street, in his own neighborhood, he'll find a way to get some trees in there before filling them back up again.

We are all paying the wages, in some way or another, of the people who manage, service, and maintain our community. These are the people who trim our trees, maintain our buildings, pave our sidewalks, patrol our streets, teach our children, and much, much more. We have not just the right, but the obligation, to ensure that we are getting the best performance from the best people.

WYNOTT EXPECT AND REWARD EXCELLENCE?

If we want excellence, we need to be willing to reward it and not punish it as we so often do.

WHAT WE BUY

One way to get the best performance from the best people is to encourage workers to live where they serve. The building manager who lives onsite knows everything that's going on every minute of the day. This might seem like it could make more work, but it makes less work because the manager develops an intuition for solving problems before they arise.

The teachers, the firefighters, and the landscapers who live in the community where they work will always know what's going on, and they take extra pride in their jobs. They will bring their highest level of service when the people that they serve are their own people. Think that sounds unreasonable? Like too much to ask? Okay, then how about we start recruiting outside of the United States for our next president? Let's open up the search worldwide and just find the most qualified candidate for the job. It shouldn't make any difference if our highest-ranked public servant lives outside of the boundary of the nation that he or she serves and commutes to work every day. A certain sense of detachment will make it easier to do the job. Right? Wrong! If you don't live in the community you serve, if you don't belong to it, it doesn't belong to you. If it doesn't belong to you, however well-meaning you are, somewhere deep down inside you just can't care for it as much.

This means that in Wynott we recruit from within the community as aggressively as possible. When that's not possible, we encourage the people hired to care for our community to move here. We offer good incentives. We like having our jobs done by our guys and our gals. We want to look them in the eye, and we want them to look us in the eye. We want to take care of our place together.

Proximity is one solution. But regardless of where workers live, they must ultimately be encouraged to give quality performance and must always be rewarded for excellence.

The bottom line is defined differently in Wynott. Our bottom line is quality of life, the health and success of our community. It doesn't always translate into dollars. If cutting a job saves money but diminishes our quality of life, that job won't be cut. That job position must, however, offer measurable results and prove its relevance. In Wynott we don't accept that "This is just the way we've always done it." Is there a better way? Things change all the time; maybe now there's a new tool or a simpler method for getting the job done. Think about it, figure it out, keep it fresh.

WHAT WE BUY

In Wynott we set goals and objectives for the people who serve us, and we encourage them to go above the call of duty to make things better. To think outside of the box. To find and implement efficiencies. To satisfy the customer. For this they will be rewarded with Wy-Notes and with public recognition.

Most people want, more than anything, to feel relevant, needed, and appreciated. When we call them out and thank them for doing good work, it makes a difference.

10

When Does It Get Better?

WYNOTT NOW!

Very early in this book we looked at the who, what, where, why, and how of Wynott. This part is the *when*. All signs point that NOW is the time for Wynott.

Facts are facts. Protection of the status quo just isn't sustainable. We can't afford to keep doing things the way they've always been done when revenues are decreasing and needs are increasing. We've simply got to figure out how to get more out of less. Every system and structure can be improved. We can solve this. All of the clues are here; we've just got to put them together.

Technology

In the Internet Age, Wikipedia, the most comprehensive and current compendium of information ever, has been freely created by unsolicited volunteers and made instantly available to the world. Think about that. What does that mean? It means that people with expertise are willing and able to share their hard-earned knowledge, with no promise of remuneration. It means that technology has advanced to the point where a small idea can take hold online and grow into a powerful force. What does this have to do with Wynott? Simply that technology makes it easier than ever for a community to come together to achieve goals. And Wikipedia proves not only that if you build it, they will come; it also proves that they will build it with you. Voluntarily.

All a Wynott community needs is a Facebook page, or something like it, with a responsible moderator, and the bulk of its people are instantly connected and able to understand a few basic facts about each other. The Internet and social networking give community members ready access to plans, as well as a simple forum to suggest new ideas and share solutions. Items can be voted on with simple polls. Anyone with an interest can say their piece, at their convenience, and know that

WELCOME TO WYNOTT

it will be read by all. If they've got something constructive to say, it will permeate. If they don't, it will be challenged and diffused, or fall flat.

The Birth of the Urban Renaissance

Across the nation, there's a movement away from suburban living and toward the rejuvenation of the city. The baby boom that built the suburbs is long over. The era of large families with stay-at-home moms has, for better or worse, passed. Several decades of census information progressively show people getting married later, starting families later, and having fewer children. The fastest-growing household type of any age is the single-person household.

Regardless of household size and makeup, the city has more action and amenities to offer than does the predictable conformity of the suburbs. Changing attitudes mean that cultural diversity can be seen as an asset and a draw, adding vibrancy to neighborhoods. New generations are less interested in living in a community where every house and every face looks exactly the same as their own. People desire more leisure time; they don't want to live miles away from their workplace and suffer a long commute. More people also work from home, spending long periods alone, and prefer being in a city where their social needs can be more easily met. People eat out more and want to live in neighborhoods with a variety of restaurants to choose from. People are seeking the urban village experience. In fact, urban village design strategies are, ironically, being incorporated into newer suburban developments in an attempt to make them feel more like the city.

Death of the SUV

Rising gas prices have made the bigger-is-better trend die down. The hottest cars on the market today are practically microscopic, with names like Mini and

Smart Car. Hybrids are saturating the streets, and auto manufacturers can't design or build alternative-powered vehicles fast enough to meet demand. People are thinking about transportation differently. More and more people are finding ways to combine fitness with transportation by biking or walking where they might once have driven. Light rail and other mass-transit projects are being green-lit and funded nationwide. People are changing the way they get around. And they're no longer willing to make the long commute, trapped behind the wheel of a gas-guzzling SUV.

The American Dream Is Changing

Owning a home doesn't mean what it used to mean. In recent years, inflated home values gave people the false confidence to withdraw equity from their homes as casually as if they were using an ATM. Now that the bubble has burst, a troubling number of Americans are "upside down" on their mortgages, meaning they owe more than the houses are actually worth. Some people are walking away from their homes and taking the loss. Others are being forced to leave by record numbers of foreclosures. It's become all too clear that the old plan of counting on your nest for a nest egg is no longer realistic. Massive shakeups in financing mean that far fewer people qualify for a mortgage. Even the best candidates who represent the lowest risk are forced to wait and jump through hoops that didn't exist just a few years ago. This crash not-so-shockingly comes on the heels of the loosest credit free-for-all in our history, where just about anyone with a pulse could get SOME kind of mortgage with no money down, no proof of employment, no accountability. But now the party is over, it's the morning after, and people have no choice but to get real. And getting real is what Wynott is all about.

The Norm Is No Longer the Norm

People just don't go with the crowd anymore. There is no defined crowd. Once-thriving institutions have been forced to streamline, reinvent themselves, or close down altogether. Consider houses of worship. There was a time when the majority of families attended a weekly service in their neighborhoods. Today, not only will people shop around for the church they like best, but they will shop around for the *religion* they like best . . . that is, if they feel they really need one, which fewer and fewer people now do.

Or take education. There was a time that, when Johnny turned five, he walked up the block to the neighborhood school. Now, by the time Johnny turns four, his parents have embarked on a lengthy fact-finding mission to learn about every public school, magnet school, charter school, alternative school, private school, and even online school vying for Johnny's attendance. If none meet Johnny's standards, well, there's always home school.

Hospitals now have marketing teams and advertising campaigns to get you through their doors. Twenty years ago, if you were having chest pains, you'd get to the nearest emergency room. Today you stop and take a precious minute or two to research which has the higher-ranked cardiology team.

People don't trust that higher powers are acting in their best interest. They want to know what's in their drinking water. Where their apples come from. If their chicken lived in a cage. What kind of meds their milk cow was on. How their coffee beans were grown, harvested, packaged, shipped, and roasted.

People no longer take institutions and systems for granted. They won't just eat what's in front of them, go where they're sent, or do what they're told. They need to know more. They want to participate. They're ready to get involved. They're asking for change.

CHA-CHA-CHA-CHANGES!

This is a book about changes, large and small. The main idea is to change the "Why?" to "Wynott!" It's pretty darn simple, when you think about it. But that doesn't mean it will be easy. Because no matter how bad things are, or how good they could be, people tend to prefer the hell they know to the hell they don't.

We do have the tools, and the choice, to stimulate change when we decide that it's good for our society. The trick with change is, people will resist it if they feel it is being imposed upon them from above. During the 1970s there was a huge push by the government—an act of Congress, as a matter of fact—to transform the way we measure ourselves as a nation. The U.S. Metric Board was formed in order to implement the Metric Conversion Act, and citizens everywhere were encouraged to abandon feet for meters, gallons for liters, and so on. Children were taught the metric system in school. Public service announcements hailed the metric system on television and billboards. It should have been a fairly simple change—just a little bit of math.

WELCOME TO WYNOTT

Americans, however, met the metric system with apathy at best and ridicule at worst. Hard to say what's so funny about being in sync with the rest of the world, especially since we're so fond of importing and exporting goods that need to be measured in universally comprehendible units. Nonetheless, in 1982 the U.S. Metric Board was disbanded.

Slowly, the Metric System did seep into our culture. Most of the products that we buy include metric measurements on the label. But decades later, new cookbooks are still being printed measuring flour in cups and vanilla in teaspoons. Lumber and fabric and other materials are still sold by the yard. Even official government drivers licenses describe the holder in pounds and inches. So much for the Metric System. The big government switchover plan was a serious flop.

Why did this seemingly logical and relatively painless change fail so spectacularly?

Let's try another example. Imagine if, back in the 1980s, the government had mandated a new system for telecommunications. By an act of Congress, all citizens were expected to unplug their trusty landlines and purchase a flimsy and fragile foreign-made cellular phone. These new, untested phones would need to be replaced, on average, every two years and would come with oppressive contract terms, costing roughly four times the amount of landlines.

WHEN DOES IT GET BETTER?

There would be rioting in the streets to prevent that kind of change. However, since the government didn't order us to do it, we've gravitated toward cell phones for what we perceive as our own convenience, despite the costs (higher bills, more frequent replacement expenses, less free time due to constant availability, increased traffic accidents, and other unknown health risks). For better or worse, we have, as a nation, achieved a dramatic fundamental shift in communication technology in less than a decade.

Here's one more example: imagine, again in the 1980s, that the leading fashion designers of the day had all gotten together and come up with an exciting new trend for their spring collection—pants that hang halfway down your bottom, leaving several inches of your underwear exposed, mimicking incarcerated gangsters not allowed to wear belts. People would have welcomed this in the same way they welcomed New Coke: with repulsion, revulsion, and ridicule. However, because this crazy pants-down trend originated bottom-up, from young urban rappers with loads of street cred, it spread. And spread. It went further than any designer could have ever hoped and lasted longer than any person over thirty could have ever stomached.

> **An act of Congress has no power compared to change that is made from the bottom up.**

WELCOME TO WYNOTT

An act of Congress has no power compared to change that is made from the bottom up. People can and do and will change. They will sometimes make positive changes to improve themselves or their world. They will try crazy things, embark on hare-brained schemes, embrace completely nutty trends. It doesn't have to make sense. *It just has to feel like a choice.*

If you really want to see something change, the best thing you can do is *do* it. Model it. Put yourself out there. Show people how it's done. Make it look cool; have an effect on your immediate circle. Get it started in your own community, then watch it ripple outward. In the words of Margaret Mead, "Never doubt that a small group of thoughtful, committed citizens can change the world. Indeed, it is the only thing that ever has."

Wynott is the home of that small group of thoughtful, committed citizens. It doesn't call for new laws or new developments. It's not a new system or a new utopia.

The ideas in this book are meant to improve current conditions, but anything could happen in the future to make some of these pages seem outdated. Even as this book is being written, the very concept of pages—of how a book is written, published, distributed, and read—is changing.

Popular fads, scientific discoveries, natural disasters, and national crises come and go, come and go. Our very bodies are in a state of flux, regenerating cell by cell, second by second. Our planet isn't fixed in place; we are a world in constant motion, spinning through an ever-expanding universe. Change is the only reliable constant.

Which is why the vital message—more important than any one idea presented here—is that we need to BUILD CHANGE INTO THE SYSTEM. Be ready for it. Watch for it. Welcome it. Because it never stops coming.

Plans, like everything else, come and go. Victor Gruen tried, with the nation's very first indoor shopping mall, to start all over with a new plan, to create an alternative to the city of Minneapolis, fixing the flaws that he felt all American cities possessed. But Gruen didn't do any better than the Levitts of Levittown did. Financially, Gruen succeeded, but that success came only with the complete reversal of his ideals and intentions.

Planned communities and utopian systems will always succumb to human error and to changing realities. Today's wisdom will often seem foolish in light of tomorrow's problems, technologies, and populations. The impulse to make things better, however, is always worthy of consideration.

In Minneapolis, just a few miles from Victor Gruen's Southdale, two vacant gas stations have languished on the intersection of 53rd Street and Nicollet Avenue South for many years. Even when boarded up and surrounded by weeds, these buildings each possessed an inherent charm.

To the north sits a cottagelike white stucco structure with a steep blue terra-cotta roof, built in the 1920s. To the south, a sleek and brash 1950s station, clad in shiny red, white, and blue metal panels, models the height of futuristic modernity in its day. These buildings have outlived their original purposes. Busy national franchise gas stations and better-known service stations now handle all of the auto business up and down Nicollet Avenue.

But instead of bringing down the value of this neighborhood, these two abandoned gas stations have been reconsidered and reinvented. Two different sets of entrepreneurs, each with more moxie than money, envisioned a new reality and transformed the gas stations into vibrant gathering spots.

First, the northern station was transformed into one of those inviting garden centers that entice people to wander around, gaze at the lush greenery and arrangements, and just breathe in the inspiration.

Across the street, the red, white, and blue gas station became a fun cafe. Working with the original service station design, the new owners created an ideal indoor/outdoor restaurant, taking advantage of the garage doors that let in light during winter and fresh air during summer.

What's most striking about the metamorphoses of these adjacent gas stations is that the new businesses

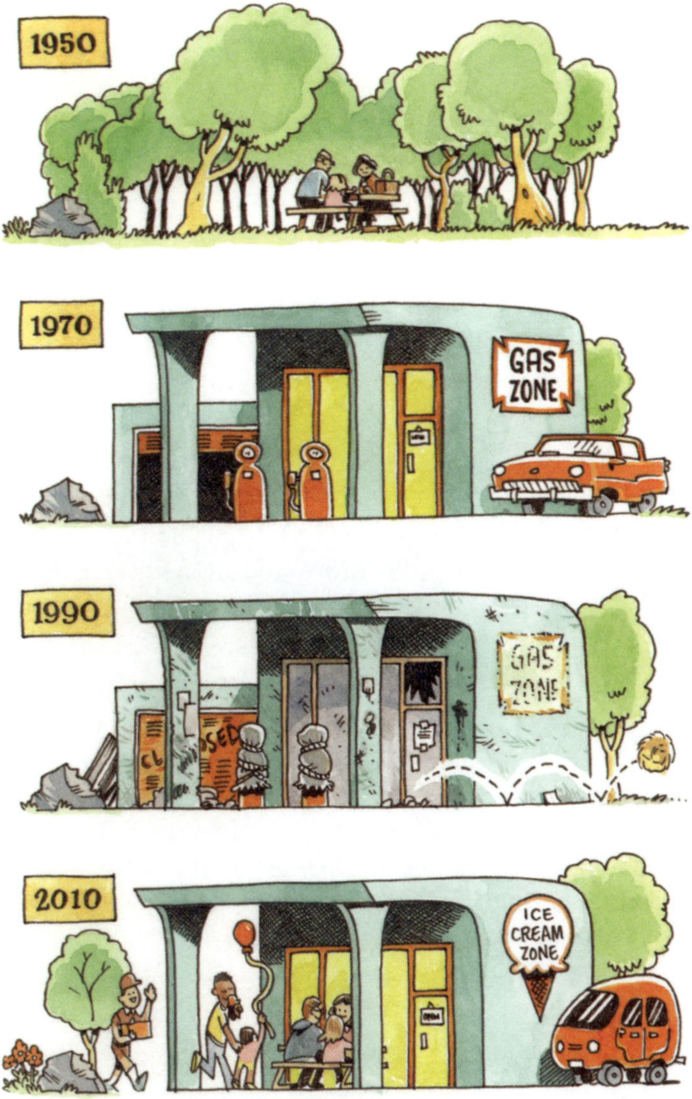
1950
1970
GAS
ZONE
1990
GAS
ZONE
2010
ICE
CREAM
ZONE

feel like they've always been there. The buildings look like they were built to spec to house a garden center and cafe. They have so quickly become relevant to this neighborhood, to each other even, that they seem to have always been part of a larger plan.

And that's what a Wynott community is. It's not a fresh new development out in the middle of a bare field somewhere, filled with idealistic recruits seeking to escape the realities of society, blindly agreeing to the false security of covenant restrictions that control their every movement.

Wynott is simply fresh thinking applied to existing places.

Wynott draws from the lessons of the past, prepares for the needs of the future, and always makes the very most of the present. It seeks out and applies best practices refined elsewhere in time and space. It's not a relic encased in amber, but rather a fluid and ever-evolving place where common sense prevails and good ideas are given the chance to flower. Or to fail. The plan for Wynott is not perfect, and is never finished. There will always be space to pencil in new realities, new solutions, new perspectives.

Things are expected to change in Wynott. Gas pumps make way for gladiolas. Empty parking lots turn into farmers markets. Tired retirees become vital volunteers. Volunteer work is made into secondary currency. Secondary currency becomes local profit.

Wynott can exist anywhere where a few people are willing to think on their feet. You just might be one of those people. What have you got in your community? You don't need to start from scratch. Look around and see what's working, what's broken. What needs to be added, renovated, updated, transformed, or phased out. Find out why things are the way they are, and then start asking "Wynott?"

Acknowledgements

It is impossible to thank all of the people throughout the years who have contributed in some way to the knowledge, the experience, and the creative impetus that led to this book. We can, however, specifically thank a small group of people who have directly supplied time and talent to make *Welcome to Wynott* a reality. For a variety of reasons, our gratitude is extended to Dara Beevas, John Lonsbury, Jay Monroe, Milt "Beaver" Adams, Doug Wallace, Red Sieve, Kathleen Fleugel, Dave Feehan, Sarah Harris, Dan Harris, Helen Metz, and Patrick Coyle.

About **Lily Coyle**

Lily Coyle is a freelance writer and playwright. She currently resides in Minneapolis with a few perfect children, an imperfect dog, and a talented husband. In writing this book, Lily was inspired by memories of her grandparents' farm, before it was sold and transformed into a suburban housing development.

Photo by Kathy Quirk-Syvertsen

About **Kevin Cannon**

Kevin Cannon is a cartoonist and illustrator whose work has appeared in children's books, graphic novels, online games, and feature films. In 2011 *City Pages* named him the "Best Cartoonist in the Twin Cities." In his free time Cannon writes and draws adventure comics, including 2009's *Far Arden*, which was nominated for an Eisner Award, the industry's highest honor. He lives in Northeast Minneapolis.